Childhood, Religion and School Injustice

Childhood, Religion and School Injustice

KARL KITCHING

CORK **cup** UNIVERSITY PRESS

First published in 2020 by
Cork University Press
Boole Library
University College Cork
Cork
T12 ND89
Ireland

Library of Congress Control Number: 2019955494
Distribution in the USA: Longleaf Services, Chapel Hill, NC, USA

British Library Cataloguing in Publication Data
A CIP record for this book is available from the British Library.

ISBN: 978-1-78205-388-0

Cover Photo: *Young Girl (iv)*, 2016, Wendy McMurdo
Printed in Poland by BZGraf
Print origination & design by Carrigboy Typesetting Services
www.carrigboy.com

www.corkuniversitypress.com

For Aoife, Niall and James, my godchildren,
and Loïc, my love. I hadn't met any of you when I started
this project. Thank you for helping me play again.

Contents

Acknowledgements

Thank you to the children, parents, principals, teachers, young people, senior citizens and religious leaders who participated in the research that underpins this book. A special word of thanks to my partner in conducting the fieldwork, Dr Yafa Shanneik, for her scholarship, sensitivity and friendship. Thanks also to Dr Gavin Deady for conducting several painstaking transcriptions.

There were ups and downs with this project due to its complexity, but also due to ill-health, which turned to disability and time away from academia. I am very privileged and grateful to have friends, colleagues and family who encouraged me, supported me with gaining access to research settings, and advised on the conceptual and practical direction of the project.

Thanks, finally, to the reviewers for their supportive analysis of this book, to the Irish Research Council for funding the research, and to Cork University Press for bringing the work to life.

Introduction

Childhood, Religion and School Injustice: Deeply Engaging Plurality?

Debate about how schools can engage a plurality of religious, spiritual and non-religious worldviews is an inherent feature of modern liberal societies. Despite the political and sometimes fraught nature of these debates, there is typically a level of public consensus about their parameters. These include (1) the state must provide some form of secular education governance to ensure freedom of expression, (2) ignoring and/or indoctrinating children is deeply unjust, and (3) multiple options, including faith formation and education about ethics and religious beliefs, are needed. Public debate about childhood, religion and schooling in Ireland, arguably, is at least as old as the 1831 colonial foundation of national (primary) schooling. For most of the nineteenth century, that debate was focused on schooling in particular religious denominations, as opposed to the question of whether religion should be addressed in school itself. But debates about religion in Irish schools, and Catholic majoritarianism specifically,

1

have intensified over the past three decades in the wake of the decline of the moral authority of the Catholic Church and successive revelations of child abuse and death in religiously governed institutions. Further pressure points in public debate have emerged more recently. These pressure points are due to poor planning for, and resourcing of, schools in residential areas, government austerity measures which have narrowed Ireland's reimagining of state-funded school governance, and ethno-religious diversification.

A significant body of scholarship has been conducted in the past twenty years, and particularly the past decade, regarding the complexities and injustices of the Catholic-dominated Irish school sector in a wider European/global context. Much of this work involves extended philosophical, legal and curricular analyses of the problems with, and possibilities of, the primary school sector and its approaches to religious education (RE). Texts such as Alison Mawhinney's *Freedom of Religion and Schools* and Eoin Daly's *Religion, Law and the Irish State* have variously dealt with legal and constitutional matters regarding religious freedom and exclusion in Irish schools.[1] *Toward Mutual Ground* and *Does Religious Education Matter?* have examined key philosophical arguments around secular/religious schooling, education about religious beliefs and ethics and faith formation.[2] Dympna Devine's *Immigration and Schooling in the Republic of Ireland* and Karin Fischer's *Schools and the Politics of Religion and Diversity* have examined the ways in which ethnicity and religion overlap and how religious and civic national worldviews permeate school curricula and policies.[3] Other edited collections such as Deegan et al.'s *Primary Voices*, Berglund et al.'s *Religious Education in a Global-Local World* and Smyth et al.'s *Religious Education in a Multicultural Europe* examine both forms of RE, and children's and parents' agency in negotiating contrasting forms of education in Ireland and Europe.[4] Eoin O'Mahony's *Religious and Secular Places* provides a crucial geography of secular–religious relations in Catholic schools as particular kinds of places.[5] Finally, Aoife Neary's *LGBT-Q Teachers, Civil Partnership and Same-Sex Marriage* examines religious patronage of schools from a queer perspective.[6]

The above texts explore to greater or lesser extents (a) the shifting, yet overlapping nature of secular, religious, majority and minority commitments in contemporary Europe, (b) the messy politics and poetics of interreligious and intercultural dialogue, (c) the need to diversify Ireland's school types and RE curricula from a children's rights perspective, and (d) how instrumental economic interests have become prioritised in global and national education policy enactments. Despite its richness, existing scholarship has not offered an integrated socio-political focus to the study of childhood, secular–religious relations, and school injustice. The book specifically contributes a critical postsecular perspective on this topic, which pushes the parameters of public debate in respect of secular education governance and childhood inequalities. This perspective challenges prevailing, unjust neoliberal and nationalist notions of secular freedom in education, which favour narrow, private self-interest, and intersecting, classed, racialised, ableist, adult-centred and gendered notions of 'good' childhoods.[7] It argues for the 'becoming public' of school systems, and for deep, affirmative engagement with plurality in schools as contested, unchosen publics.

Against Neoliberal, Ethno-Nationalist Governance and Notions of Freedom

One of the greatest challenges of engaging religious, spiritual and non-religious worldviews in modern societies is that perceived differences in worldviews can be overemphasised, to the point of encouraging competitive claims to the truth, and racialised, class and gendered views of what it means to be free. Such challenges are exacerbated by contemporary neoliberal and nationalist ideologies and governing logics. As Rosi Braidotti argues, neoliberalism and nationalism do not necessarily or solely seek to supress difference – they exploit its power. In neoliberal and nationalist political, social, institutional and economic contexts, 'difference is essentialized'.[8] This means that internal differences and nuances within social groups tend to be either suppressed, or exploited for marketing purposes, with the effect of hierarchising certain forms of identity, worldview and concepts of freedom.

Neoliberalism (or post-neoliberalism) is an inherently amorphous toolkit for enacting policy in the context of re-entrenched, 'post-austerity' racialised capitalism.[9] Since the global financial crisis, neoliberalism has taken on somewhat new manifestations. It both facilitates white national protectionist 'freedoms', and liberal free-trade ideals, which encourage the attraction of 'good' migrants.[10] In this book, I discuss how neoliberal education policy enactments exploit, align and/or oppose religious, spiritual and non-religious worldviews, for the purposes of privatising and/or marketising schools. Processes of privatisation and marketisation seek to shape competing, active parent consumer-citizens who 'appropriately' develop children. In so doing, such processes maintain or exacerbate class, race

4

and gender-related advantages and injustices. Neoliberal policy enactments support the branding of schools into neat, secular/religious categories. This branding undermines engagement with the messiness of secular–religious relations as a *public* education concern.

Neoliberalism also inherits a colonial impulse that encourages us to calculate what we are getting from a worldview, thus undermining the key role that collective wonder, creativity and shared obligations play in our encounters with others.[11] As a policy and political toolkit, it conflates secular personal freedoms with individual (adult) self-interest and ignores the unchosen complexities and attachments of our socio-religious, classed, racialised and gendered experience.

Various forms of nationalism, rigid communitarianism and their oppression of minorities are not simply 'resurgent' or confined to Brexit Britain and Trump's America. Gerardine Meaney argues that Ireland's Catholic moral communitarianism and its promulgation of the Virgin Mary was linked to a nationalist 'compensatory urge to promote an essential Irishness that was purer – in effect whiter – than other European races'.[12] As Neera Chandhoke outlines, the contemporary power of extreme right-wing Hindu nationalist movements in India underlines the importance of not taking for granted the basic secular freedom to express one's worldview – particularly for minoritised groups.[13] In western Europe, a 2018 Pew study found that 54 per cent of practising and 48 per cent of non-practising Christians agreed 'our people are not perfect, but our culture is superior to others';[14] 42 per cent of the total Irish sample agreed with this 'superior' statement. Unsurprisingly then, in supposedly liberal national contexts, casually racist and absolutist truth-claims permeate apparently sensible public discourses on the nation's children and, in particular, their consumption practices. For example, corporate media and reality TV representations in the UK and Ireland routinely frame Traveller and white working-class families as too materialist, not authentically religious, unfree, or free in the wrong ways.[15] In Ireland and Europe's pre- and post-austerity politics, those who do not appear to embody or reproduce 'free' secular-rationalist, racialised, classed, ableist, adult-centred and gendered ideals of normal and proper childhoods are classified as a burden, as social failures, and/or as a threat to 'our' freedom.[16]

What are we to do then, if, as Braidotti asserts:

> The much-celebrated phenomenon of globalization and of its technologies . . . combines the euphoric celebration of *new* technologies, *new* economy, *new* life styles . . . with the utter social rejection of change . . . the consumerist and socially enhanced faith in the *new* is supposed not only to fit in with but also actively to induce the rejection of in-depth change.[17]

My goal in this book is not only to challenge neoliberal and (white, Christian) nationalist notions of secular freedom, but to outline a critical postsecular understanding of childhood, religion and school injustice that supports school systems in processes of 'becoming public'.[18] This perspective argues that, acknowledging there is no universal template on which to build a public school system, we must (1) challenge, in context-relevant ways, the overwhelming privatisation and marketisation of school systems as a public political act/concern, (2) dispense with assumptions of education policy's secular neutrality, which undermine minority religious and ethical school movements that do not have the same capacity to gain an implicit 'market

6

share' and (3) educationally and socially engage the plural child, in a way that challenges multiple forms of injustice in childhood (racialised, classed, ableist, gendered, religious) and admits that there is no universal template for what a good childhood should be. I regard it as possible and necessary to articulate and map critical postsecular principles for deep, public, creative engagement with plurality across multiple contexts. These principles encourage engagement with the everyday ways that children's and adults' unique ideas, bodies and identities are captured by, but may also escape, calculating, narrow self-interest, ethno-nationalism, and dichotomous, secular/religious ideas of what a good or authentic childhood or school is. In developing this critical postsecular perspective, I argue that the plurality of contested, unchosen school publics (presented in this book) past, present and future helps us think in more nuanced ways about issues surrounding childhood, religion and school injustice.

Deeply Engaging Plurality: Nuance and Complexity Over Rigid Notions of Difference

This book examines religion as a social activity, and is not theological in emphasis or approach. Of course, I recognise that while religious practices are earthly creations, 'the cultural forms of religion . . . may or may not be divinely inspired'.[19] As postcolonial scholarship underlines, it is epistemically false and unjust for me, particularly as a white, male, western, Catholic-raised, agnostic adult, to claim to give voice here to the religious, spiritual, non-religious experience of marginalised, child others.[20]

The book is not framed by a rationalist, essentialist model of the western secular-modern child, around which all other childhoods must revolve, and for whom the same experiences are always due. Nor do I claim that I can satisfactorily translate or re-present religious, spiritual and non-religious traditions and experiences of other children or adults. Rather, as referenced above, I seek to support public educational understandings of *the plural child*, who encounters the world in complex, ongoing ways that are irreducible to absolute truth claims (including those of religion, science and even reason and rights). Children are not blank canvases upon which society, schools or particular worldviews reproduce their own image of what is good. But neither are they autonomous actors. As chapters four and five explore, through their encounters with human and non-human others (including spaces, objects, ideas), children continuously generate and/or shut down new forms of ethical relations and accountability.

The term 'plurality' as used in this book does not refer to religions, ethnicities, or bodies that operate as entirely separate, autonomous entities that can be counted and commodified by policy discourse. Nor does it refer solely to religious, spiritual and non-religious worldviews. Rather plurality refers to qualitative, conscious and unconscious processes of encounter and mutual shaping between human and non-human (material, cultural and supernatural) entities. This understanding of plurality has implications for how we understand traditional secular freedoms and ethics, as discussed later. The book's critical postsecular focus on generating specific forms of openness to plural, ongoing encounters with human and non-human others does not ignore the specificity of personal or organised religious, spiritual and non-religious worldviews. Rather it seeks to deepen

8

understanding of their complexity, and each person's singularity, in affirmative, constructive ways. As discussed throughout, I refute the idea that there is a uniform, ideal public sphere or neutrally secular form of education governance through which governing logics of market choice, competition, self-reliance, managerialism or reanimated spirits of sectarianism and nationalism can be vanquished. I do not assume that any master narrative or ideal based in religion, civil religious education, civic nationalism, science, reason, human rights or anything else can offer clear, universal common ground or absolute freedom to educators, children or families. Rather I contend we must take the reality of complex, contested, unchosen and unequal school publics and the everyday opening up and closing down of forms of ethical relations and accountability as a touchstone for transnational, socially just imaginings and engagements of childhood, religion and schooling, across multiple settings.

Paraphrasing Bronwyn Davies,[21] our entanglements with emotion, memory, place and objects exceed prevailing, individualist and binary (secular/religious; authentic/inauthentic; public/private) notions of what a desirable good school or free childhood is. The good news, then, is that schools and childhoods are not solely sites of commodification, majoritarianism, securitisation or nationalism: they are postsecular sites of imagination, wonder, messiness, experimentation and collectivity. In order to deeply engage with the plurality of schools and childhoods, I argue we need to meaningfully, empirically engage the complexities of children's and adults' everyday socio-religious encounters with the world. After Avery Gordon,[22] this involves dealing with the ghosts, silences and omissions that modern societies create. We need to engage memories of our own childhoods – and how histories

9

of joyful, positive, negative and painful school experiences may impede us, or open us up to others, including to future, unknowable generations. In a complex, consumerist world, our ideas, identities and bodies are messy, that is, 'simultaneously disposable commodities to be vampirised and also decisive agents for political and ethical transformation'.[23] Echoing Ghassan Hage and Rosi Braidotti,[24] I combine the desire to critique unjust circumstances in different school contexts with affirmatively mapping alternative childhoods and cultivating ways of doing school that insist and persist alongside and underneath our taken-for-granted ways of living and being with each other.

Postsecular Childhoods: Researching White, Irish, Catholic School Majoritarianism

What does the term 'postsecular' refer to? Perhaps appropriately, there is no great consensus on what the term means, or how conceptually useful it is.[25] I use the term as a way of thinking about the entanglements of the secular and the religious in virtually every element of the social. Habermas coined the concept of a 'postsecular' Europe to mark the 'return' of religion to this political arena. Braidotti et al. argue that there was no neatly secular European public space to which religion has returned as a matter of concern.[26] As Gurminder K. Bhambra discusses, modern Europe was always already plural and unequal, not least due to its colonising projects and ties.[27] Not only did religion never leave European public spheres, Braidotti et al. argue that there continues to be a Christian-centred consensus embedded in Habermas' hailing of a postsecular Europe. This consensus assumes, among other things, that:

> Secularism both as an institutional practice – the separation of state from church – and as a philosophical frame is a distillation of Judeo-Christian precepts, notably respect for the law, for the intrinsic worth of the individual person, the autonomy of the self, moral conscience, rationality, and the ethics of love . . . In other words, the Christian faith allows for rational thought, based on a teleological or evolutionary vision of the future and on humanist faith in human reason's capacity to self-regulate and steer social progress.[28]

The assumptions above facilitate a western, Eurocentric, Christian and rationalist understanding of secular freedom and progress, which fail to account for the central role that anti-colonial, anti-racist, feminist and LGBTQ movements amongst others have played in transnational struggles for emancipation and justice. Secular principles have been importantly (if unevenly) central to mass education governance since the early nineteenth century. But the idea that western secular modernity is a universal, or entirely desirable, human experience disregards its emergence through colonial, capitalist, racist structures and their manifestation in legacies such as Ireland's patron-based, effectively privatised approach to state-funded schooling. Given the complex forms of domination and struggle that secular modernity has given rise to, there is no one blueprint for contemporary secular–religious relations, or for what a 'secular' school or public space is. Rather, 'the postsecular condition is diverse, multicultural, and internally differentiated'.[29] The postsecular is not, then, a period 'after' secularism as such.

It is rather a perspective on the world which recognises the complex entanglement of the secular and religious in all aspects of the social. It refuses narrow western framings of European societies as beacons of secular political progress, challenges multiple injustices of colonial capitalism and racial neoliberalism, and explores what can emerge/be created from the failure of religion, rights, reason or science to provide absolute, universal common ground for public education.

Drawing on Rosi Braidotti's work, a form of faith in, or 'residual spirituality' in critical theory and the need to formulate socially just imaginaries drives this work.[30] The book's critical postsecular perspective is not a rationalist or neutral view from nowhere: it is entirely indebted to feminist poststructural, postcolonial and posthuman scholarship. The book grounds its critical postsecular perspective in an empirical study of childhood and schooling in the Republic of Ireland. There are just over 3,000 mainstream state-funded primary schools in Ireland;[31] 90 per cent of state-funded primary schools are Catholic-run. I use the Irish context as a case study to critique injustice and think affirmatively about deep engagement with plurality, in ways that should resonate across multiple education settings transnationally.

Ireland's contemporary policies on school provision work to intensify competition among different religious and secular school patrons, at the expense of considering the damage of austerity measures to our ethical imagination. Such market-led policies, which are reflected across the globe, have key social costs.[32] They advantage historically dominant, organised worldviews in school systems. In Ireland, for example, the Catholic church has greater material resources – at least in property terms – to offer school places, and to recast 'tradition' and 'community' as commodities. Contemporary education policy on new and changing school populations in Ireland also pits school patrons, and the secular/religious worldviews they represent, against each other. A recent (April 2019) example of this was the scaremongering used by three northeast Dublin Catholic primary school authorities, to undermine a potential shift to a secular school ethos and patron body for one of the eight Catholic schools in the area.[33]

Sacramental preparation for first communion and confirmation is the norm in Ireland's Catholic schools. Thus, the majority of children in Ireland either participate in, or witness first communion preparation at school, making it an important thread woven throughout the book. The data generated with children and adults in this book forms part of a large qualitative study of childhoods and socio-religious change funded by the Irish Research Council. The study was called 'Making Communion: Disappearing and Emerging Forms of Childhood in Ireland'. Dr Yafa Shanneik (now at the University of Birmingham) and I conducted much of the fieldwork for this study together. Yafa's expertise and engagement with participants was vital, and she has since co-edited the book, *Religious Education in a Global-Local World*, as one strand of her scholarship since the project.[34] The study involved 172 participants aged between 6 and 92 years across four rural, town, suburban and city school localities of mixed social-class status. The aim of the project was to examine children's, young people's, parents', teachers', clerics' and senior citizens' experiences of childhood, and to deconstruct first communion as a normative symbol of Irishness.

The bulk of the fieldwork involved over 100 seven–eight-year-old children in classroom art and drama-based activities, and photo and video response techniques in friendship-based, small-group settings. Most of these children attended second class (the fourth year of primary school in Ireland), where preparation for first communion during school hours is the norm in the majority of schools. The majority of children were white, settled, Irish and of Catholic heritage. A significant minority of children, particularly in the Educate Together setting, were of minority ethnic and religious backgrounds. Due to challenges in accessing schools that would explicitly identify as serving Traveller families (itself indicative of systemic racism), we engaged with a Traveller Community Development organisation for some limited data collection. Here, we interviewed two Traveller boys, two young women and two older adults. We also consulted the parish of the Travelling People. While clearly children with disabilities and different abilities were part of every school, an explicit sampling for, and focus on, dis/ability was not part of the scope of the study. As chapters three and six show, we conducted a range of group and individual interviews with adults in nine schools across the localities, focusing on experiences of childhood, religion and schooling.

The empirical data analysed in chapters four and five demonstrate how ambiguity, difference and indifference are at play amidst the religious attachments of children of different backgrounds, including children raised in Catholic school and familial settings. However, in the context of this book's argument for schools becoming public, I do not assume that Catholicism in Ireland is on the way out, or that Irish society is progressing because of certain dynamics of religious decline and change.[35] This secularist assumption helps reinforce the tendencies of certain Catholic advocates to present institutional Catholicism in Ireland as a victim, and to hold tighter to exclusionary school majorities. Assumptions that religiosity will inevitably die out does not support Irish society to confront with its own postsecular condition: schools must (and do) engage with the ongoing reality of plural, deeply held worldviews.[36] We must engage and build public educational capacities to encounter deeply embodied commitments, ambiguity, wonder and mystery within and across worldviews, and challenge injustices which deny or stigmatise specifically minoritised groups within the school system and public discourse.

Given the demographic of the participants, the book's examination of injustice focuses particularly on intersections of children's and adults' religious/spiritual/non-religious worldview with advantages and disadvantages related to their social class, race/ethnicity, gender and age/generation. The study admittedly did not originate with a clearly defined, critical postsecular perspective. The data generated with adults and children was so wide-ranging that it required significant further development and analysis, leading ultimately to the two lenses further outlined below. My aim in further outlining these overlapping lenses is that they will help us to better understand and analyse children's and adults' experiences, and to further support robust, creative and critical engagement with plurality.

Postsecular perspective 1: The plural child, secular agency and unequal childhoods

Davis argues, provocatively, that Childhood Studies has secularised our understanding of childhood.[37] He contends that studies of childhood have placed:

at the heart of scholarly and moral attention a sternly scientific project of understanding, intervention and inclusion . . . purging it of those geneaological markers such as 'innocence', 'incapacity', 'dependence', 'wonder'.

15

Davis' argument, while critiquing positivist/scientific scholarly framings of childhood, fails to recognise a range of feminist theological, poststructural and postdevelopmental scholarship that explores complex child experiences of innocence and experience, wonder and knowing.[38] It does, however, have merit in challenging the tendency of mainstream social research's to not focus on collective wonder in childhood, and its failure to challenge separations of the human 'I', which is singular, from 'society', which is plural. One of the key elements of the book's critical postsecular perspective is to challenge the secularist, western, individualised model of the child, which underpins racialised, ableist, classed and gendered understandings of 'good' childhoods, and which ironically, ignores shared and interdependent experiences of agency/freedom. Bronwyn Davies argues:

> This individualized subject is understood as an active agent and the construction of it as such within western cultures is so pervasive that it is difficult to think against the grain of it, or to imagine that agency might indeed be blocked by this constitution of subjects as individualized identities.[39]

Due to its focus on the individualised subject, mainstream Childhood Studies has not comprehensively examined how children's lives are subject to nuanced religious and secular relations, and experiences of freedom and agency. Understanding the child/person as composed by plural encounters with the world, as multiply shaped by race, class and gender advantage/injustice, and as entangled in messy secular–religious relations and forms of freedom is crucial to this book's critical postsecular perspective.

The secularist individualisation of agency as located primarily in one worldview – for example, rights, reason, or science – can also limit how we understand what it means to be free. For example, the 'secular theology' that we have competing individual rights to interpret religious symbols is not a neutral understanding of freedom and dependence. It is a culturally specific understanding. It is linked to a Eurocentric understanding of religiosity as 'a set of propositions to which the individual gives consent'.[40] As Saba Mahmood argued, this understanding of religion ignores religious 'attachment and cohabitation' with images, icons and symbols in various religious and philosophical traditions, where the power of an object may lie in its capacity to allow each person to find for themselves 'a structure that has bearing on how one conducts oneself in this world'.[41] In a linked manner, Cooey suggests that a fundamental contradiction occurs in legal rulings in the US context, where the wishes of parents who refuse blood transfusions for their child on religious grounds are not recognised.[42] She argues that this contradiction occurs because such rulings typically view children as incapable of religious commitments:

> The child's neutrality is actually its imposed secularity, its value that of a potential adult who may one day choose religiosity, largely understood as holding to a belief, a set of beliefs, or a worldview; for the moment the child can be considered only in terms of preserving its materiality, often of secondary importance to its religious community.[43]

Capacities to be devout, or more broadly committed, then, can involve forms of habituated, affective embodied practice that (a) involves, but is not reducible to singular individual agency or meaning-making, and (b) emphasises, but is not reducible to, embodied, felt entanglement and interdependency with material culture (clothing, icons, visuals etc.).[44] The notion of competing individual rights to internally 'assign' meanings to things cannot entirely appreciate freedoms which come in the form of multiple, embodied forms of religiosity, commitment and interdependency.

My point here is not to assume that religiosity and law are incompatible, or to say that interventions (such as blood transfusions) should never take place. I do not abandon the truth-claims of rights (law) or science (medicine), but recognise how their *particular* deployment may erase children's embodied plurality and complexity. We need to avoid reducing the 'I' to being singular, and seeing only society as plural. The book's critical postsecular perspective requires an understanding of the person that is less vulnerable to neoliberal and nationalist emphases on narrow self-interest. This perspective imaginatively engages the plurality of each child/person, by examining collective, human and non-human relations that place *encounters*, and not the isolated human, at the centre of public questions of agency and accountability. Understanding the child as plural involves shifting our understanding of agency as the collective *becoming* of, as appropriate, human, non-human and supra-human forces.

Empirical research informed by the work of Gilles Deleuze and Karen Barad on 'becoming' and 'intra-action' is helpful in explaining the educational possibilities of understanding the plural child. Anna Hickey-Moody's work in particular draws on arts practices with children to examine 'intra-active' faith: 'faiths coming together to make new beliefs about what religion could be'.[45] Here, everyday engagement with plurality is a multifaceted, affective process of encounter within and across bodies, ideas, objects and places, with socially imaginative consequences. These ideas do not seek to undermine deeply held convictions, commitments or identities. Rather they affirmatively explore such commitments in their complexity and entanglement, beyond individualist notions of the self. Davies asserts this is a deeply ethical perspective:

> My emphasis on openness to becoming different in one's encounters does not run against or deny the very specificity of the person, or the longing each one of us has to be recognized in that specificity. Rather, I am suggesting the very specificity of the individual is *mobile* and *intra-active*; in each encounter we are affected by the other (Lenz Taguchi, 2010). Our capacity to enter into encounters, to recompose ourselves, to be affected, enhances our specificity and expands our capacity for thought and action (Dahlberg and Moss, 2005).[46]

Every research encounter with children in this study raised ethical questions about how we are, and could be, accountable to each other, often in ways that could not be reduced to pre-existing language, to individual agency, fixed social categories, or to a particular worldview based in reason, religion, or science. Below, I engaged in a thought experiment with white Irish Catholic six- and seven-year-olds in a rural Catholic school as part of the fieldwork. We considered a possible future, where first communion does not, or might not, happen for them. This discussion happened somewhat furtively, while the school principal, who welcomed our work, was at the other end of the room teaching small learning support groups.

Karl:	What if you didn't make your [first] communion next year, what would happen?
Max:	You get fired from the school. [everyone laughs]
Brendan:	I will? [Max laughs]
Sasha:	How do you know, because in the future – you can't read the future
Karl:	Who decides that they do or don't do it?
Max:	Myself.
Sasha:	Parents.
Brendan:	Maybe both of them. Maybe we will have a vote.
Karl:	What reasons would someone vote yes or no?
Brendan:	Because I want to be holy.
Sasha:	You get the bread of life.
Karl:	Oh what's that?
Sasha:	A piece of bread.
Brendan:	And wine.
Max:	And whiskey!
Karl:	Is it just bread like you get in the shop?
Sasha:	It kind of looks like a button . . . white buttons.
Brendan:	You know the buttons that you eat . . . you can get white chocolate buttons too.

Unlikely images, laughs and utterances intra-acted, and did not follow an orderly pattern in this research encounter, as with most others. Questions about what is real and symbolic, sacred and non-sacred, were unintentionally explored here, not simply through language (which might reduce us to rigid categories of the secular and religious), but through affectively powerful images of wine, whiskey, buttons and bread. Unique imaginings of the principal as employer, family as a democracy (which votes on whether their child becomes holy through the bread of life [eucharist]), the potency of alcoholic drinks, the pleasure of white chocolate and the indeterminacy of holy bread as being part of God's body all emerge.

Above, to quote Maggie MacLure, 'bodies and things do not confront one another as constants but are articulated as sense'.[47] The point of engaging 'nonsense' as the accompaniment to linguistic sense is that it recognises that bodies and things – including worldviews – are in a constant process of transition (becoming and intra-action), and are affected by things that, before our encounters, we may not even realise are involved. This approach to analysis complicates, rather than trivialises, deep convictions, responsibilities and commitments. Being open to that which is opaque, unexpected and difficult to name in both ourselves and others, as Judith Butler argues (via Levinas), is a key basis for ethical accountability.[48] Our experience of the world and of our own life stories is often messy, involving past and future imaginaries, relationships and experiences of joy and suffering. Drawing on Kathryn Bond Stockton's work, I argue later that engagement with plurality involves children and adults 'growing sideways'.[49] In brief, 'growing sideways' refers here to connecting intergenerationally on our multiple experiences of pleasure, pain, joy, sadness, knowing and uncertainty, to find ways around linear, often judgemental notions of children 'growing up' to reproduce societal ideals. 'Growing sideways' is entirely linked to the concept of the creative, plural child/person.

At the same time as I describe the child in a critical postsecular perspective as plural and becoming, I refer to childhoods as unequal. Indeed, challenging the privileges that variously white, settled, middle-class Catholic adults and children enjoy over others in Ireland's school system is a central task of the work. Chapters three and four, for example, demonstrate ways in which advantaged children's encounters with the world may close down new ethical relations with others. Admittedly, the book does not foreground the differences in formal religious observance and literacy between many white, settled, Irish Catholic families and others in the context of a Catholic majority school sector. But this decision is not to suggest that the issue of religious literacy and observance is unimportant to the discussion of public school provision: quite the opposite. The critical postsecular perspective outlined here seeks to emphasise intra-active encounters over measuring pre-defined levels of religiosity, spirituality or non-religiosity for a particular reason. Children's encounters with the world involve differential experiences of knowing, not-knowing, enjoyment, pain, belonging and exclusion. Examining the plurality and creativity inherent to our encounters is one part of the process of affirmatively imagining just, public educational alternatives to monolithic, unjustly institutionalised worldviews, privatised schooling and stigmatised childhoods. Cultivating and supporting this way of knowing can help challenge the dichotomising of majority/minority and secular/religious worldviews and enable us to think about childhood and adulthood in education in terms of cross-cutting, interdependent minorities, situated within complex, unchosen school publics.[50]

Postsecular perspective 2: Contested, unchosen school publics

The idea of common schooling, where children learn *about* religions rather than *through* them in their own locality, has a long, but largely diluted and downplayed history in Ireland. As submissions to Ireland's Forum on Patronage and Pluralism almost a decade ago showed, some arguments for radically overhauling Ireland's sectarian, segregated school patronage system leaned towards, or were in favour of, an entirely secular common school system.[51] There are many aspects to the common school view that are crucial to fight for, for the deep engagement of plurality. Systematic education about worldviews other than one's own typically helps develop a critical understanding of the complexity of understanding others, while also helping construct a positive, shared orientation towards doubt and ambiguity within one's own worldview.[52] Ash Amin regards schools as potential micropublics, and argues that their effectiveness:

> lies in placing people from different backgrounds in new settings where engagement with strangers in a common activity disrupts easy labelling of the stranger as enemy and initiates new attachments. They are moments of cultural destabilization.[53]

Amin uses the term 'micropublics' to refer to urban settings where everyday, mundane cross-cultural engagement and negotiation is unavoidable.[54] But, he notes, if spaces such as schools 'come segregated at the start, the very possibility of everyday contact with difference is cut out'.[55] Movements for public, common, secular schooling as a space for engagement with multiple forms of difference are important, but they are inevitably messy and complex.[56] They can and do include religious communities and learning about and from religions. The key challenge in Ireland is, as this book examines, that Catholic schooling has structurally and historically defined the public to be educated. Certainly, at curriculum and management level, the definition of the public in conservative Catholic communitarian terms has unravelled, slowly and unevenly. O'Mahony contends that, while local school patronage in Ireland

23

remains the key way a community of interest in the education field is spatialised or defined, Catholic schools have 'moved from being a local resource to being re-spatialised through understandings of citizenship, rights and civil society'.[57] This is emphasised in the Catholic RE curriculum, for example, in terms of participation and inter-religious literacy.[58] At the same time, Catholic devotion amongst those responsible for upholding the ethos and curriculum of Catholic schools varies, and is highly personalised, for example, amongst newly qualifying teachers.[59] Thus, O'Mahony makes the crucial point that, while such schools 'are changing from being places of religious catechesis into ones of a more varied public, who forms this public becomes an important question'.[60] Byrne and Devine's research on Catholic second-level schools in this context is useful in explaining the intensity of faith and religious practices in a marketised context.[61]

In market-oriented, privatised education systems, the assumption that there is clearly defined public to be educated is deeply compromised. Today's defining of the public to be educated primarily as consumer-citizens ignores middle-class white, settled, Irish Catholic dominance of secular–religious relations in Ireland's school localities. Here, parents' capacity to maintain or mobilise their ethno-religious classed, racialised and gendered interests regarding their children's development can act as relatively unconscious or conscious, partial or total proxies for their orientation towards a particular secular or religious school. The notion that there is a unitary phenomenon called 'public reason' enabled through education and equally accessible to all is thus deeply flawed. As Nancy Fraser has argued, there is no such thing as an equally accessible, monolithic public sphere. Indeed, feminism has shown how problematic the public/private distinction lying behind this monolithic notion of one public is. Minoritised groups such as women, working classes and ethnic minorities form their own overlapping, plural counterpublics and, as Nira Yuval-Davis shows, associated claims to citizenship.[62] Indeed, the ways that mothers in particular negotiate unchosen, unequal school localities in this regard is examined in chapter two.[63]

Do children form a recognised part of varied publics in and around schools? Policy rhetoric suggests that they do, but the reality is, as ever, complex and context-dependent. Qvortrup argues that child-aged persons were, paradoxically, much more visible in public in premodernity, when the concept of childhood did not exist. This shifted in modernity, towards children becoming confined to the family and school. Here, children obtained something of a greater say in the more confined sphere of schooling, and the private sphere of the home.[64] However, through forms of art, protest, sport and other activities, children and young people also certainly participate in what Anna Hickey-Moody refers to as 'little public spheres'. Such publics 'articulate the expression of youth voice in the many political tones it can have', where 'public agendas such as those around health and wellbeing coexist with the private practices of youth who articulate or resist these agendas'.[65]

If there is no universal public sphere or ideal, static, normative, common ground to be found, then, how are we to think about shared ethics and commonality in education? As the previous subsection argues, ethically centring the complex encounters of human and non-human entities is crucial. Homi Bhabha argues for a fluid, contingent, affective ethics of commonality, focusing on shifting historical locations, interrelations, problems, becomings, and belongings, rather than placing an individualised self, located at the middle of ideal-type, static, presumed moral communities of the family, neighbourhood, country and globe.[66] Drawing on Adrienne Rich's poem 'Eastern Wartime', Bhabha shows the secular-liberal imagining of the individual 'I' who is affiliated to various static, 'concentric' and ideal-type moral communities to be problematic. The lesson is that our pursuit of school publics must be responsive to shifting and plural modes of becoming family, school, Irish, and human, and how these modes are (re)formed in exclusionary ways under racial neoliberalism. In terms of centring childhood, there is no question about the need to both enable and protect children. But universalist notions of child development and human progress fail to engage with the lived ethics of childhoods and multiple becomings/trajectories of development. I explore this further in chapters one, four and six.

I describe all state-funded school localities in this book as contested, unchosen publics, for a number of reasons. First, framing state-funded, national curriculum focused school settings as *publics* is an important analytic and normative commitment towards generating new social imaginaries and supporting education and social movements, even if most schools in Ireland are *quasi*-public, that is, framed by patronage and religious (Catholic) traditions. Second, the terms 'contested' and 'unequal' indicate that school public(s) cannot be reduced to an entirely equal, universally subscribed to, singular secular or religious school community. Lily Kong argues we must acknowledge 'simultaneous, fluctuating and conflicting investment of sacred (that is, religious) and secular meanings on any one site'.[67] Primary schools are thus settings where relationships between secular and religious meanings

26

and commitments are negotiated and contested on an inter- and intra-generational basis. Third, the term 'unchosen' refers to the fact that there is little personal freedom in Ireland's existing school landscape for minority religious and non-religious children and families. But more fundamentally, it challenges majoritarian, neoliberal policy discourses of self-interested school choice, and emphasises the possibilities inherent in our unchosen, public obligations to known and unknown others.[68]

Fourth, the term 'contested' is a reference to religious, racialised and other injustices and contingent, agonistic and sometimes antagonistic relationships that exist within and between families, school staff, education policy-makers and different community representatives in school localities. 'Contested' also refers to the difficulty of ever neatly defining schools as (a) secular/religious and (b) *either* learning spaces which provide children with respite from politics, *or* spaces that are overtly political and public spheres of deliberation. Using an either/or understanding of schools as pedagogical/ political is unhelpful. In schools and child cultures, the exchange of knowledge and experience is shaped both by everyday mundane power relations, and parliamentary deliberations. Echoing Biesta, we need to think about the 'becoming public' of schools. Public pedagogy:

> neither teaches nor erases the political by bringing it under the regime of learning, but rather opens up the possibility for forms of human togetherness through which freedom can appear . . . which contribute to the 'becoming public' of spaces and places.[69]

The term 'contested' is regarded here as affirmative, where mappings of otherness 'prompts, mobilizes, and allows for flows of affirmation of values and forces which are not yet sustained by the current conditions'.[70] Fifth, while proximal (home, school, neighbourhood) relationships are hugely significant to our experience of the world, defining schools as *'micro*-publics' inadvertently suggests that national and global socio-political dynamics have an only peripheral influence on child and adult lives, and that we do not engage with such dynamics in everyday ways. Ultimately, this analysis of contested, unchosen school publics shows that discussions of the public-to-be-educated can never be held at an abstract level. They must be grounded in the embodied, material realities of place, timetabling and a variety of dynamics of tradition, resistance, commodification and creativity. In other words, they must engage a plurality of overlapping and contested publics and complex, unequal childhoods.

Outline of Chapters One to Six

Chapter one: Understanding worldviews and placing 'Irish' childhoods and schools

The following chapter further unpacks most of the above, admittedly condensed, ideas and arguments, and gives them room to breathe in various ways. Chapter one (a) clarifies my use of the term 'religious, spiritual and non-religious worldviews', (b) places childhood historically and considers the ethical possibilities of children and adults 'growing sideways' to work around the reproductive, rigid tendencies of majoritarian cultures, (c) maps some detail of Ireland's colonial and neoliberal geographies of schooling in Ireland and children's identities and forms of citizenship in those contexts, and (d) summarises some key critical postsecular principles for deep political engagement with plurality in movements supporting the becoming public of schools. I argue that in order for deep engagement with plurality to be advanced, debates on schooling and religion need to go beyond engaging children's religious, spiritual and non-religious worldviews. We also need to challenge the reproduction of classed, racialised, ableist and gendered child development ideals, and age-based, neoliberal pressures on both children and adults to act appropriately. This chapter calls for engagement of presumptive generosity towards others – but particularly those excluded on the basis of age, gender, race, religion, class, sexual orientation and dis/ability. Engagement with plurality must not happen solely through policy rhetoric, but by acknowledging school localities in the present as contested, unchosen and unequal publics, where difficult and uncomfortable feelings are affirmatively engaged. However, the process of imagination and change is vexed, as chapter two explores.

Chapter two: Contested, unchosen school publics: Parents negotiating school 'choice'

Chapter two demonstrates the feelings that emerge from the fact that there is no such thing as religious or non-religious neutrality and universal common ground in education governance. The chapter argues that the principles expressed in global and Irish education policy discourse regarding secular school provision (for example, human rights, diversity, choice) cannot be viewed as abstract ideas with fixed, universally agreed meanings and liberating potential. This is because neoliberal education policy enactments successfully merge contradictory values and ideas in order to privatise schooling and create and expand school markets.

I move to analyse interviews with adults from the four primary-school localities (with nine schools in total) that are the focus of this book. I examine how parents and school staff encounter, shape and become shaped by multiple contradictory factors regarding 'choice' of school. Each school setting reflects overlapping, contested and unchosen publics, formed partly through classed, racialised and gendered degrees of family mobility and Catholic majoritarianism. Interviews demonstrate that the configuration of secular–religious relations in these school localities is complex, place-specific, and connected into national and global contestations of the meaning of secular governance, citizenship and belonging. In order to cultivate deep engagement with plurality in education policy discourse and everyday schooling, I argue in this chapter that the policy fantasy of a self-interested Irish citizenry, freely and equally competing for their choice of school, needs to be challenged by education and social movements in a more sustained manner. Conceptualisation of and engagement with complex, contested, unchosen and unequal publics in policy discourse and policy enactments is crucial.

Chapter three: Children, worldviews and plurality: Growing sideways

Children in both formally secular and religious schools must negotiate a number of different paradoxes. Alexander notes a paradox in the liberal stance that in order to encourage freedom of conscience, those freedoms must be restricted to particular forms of education.[71] Yet this implies, inadvertently, that children are on a linear trajectory – from being unknowing to knowing – with regard to the school's ethos. Chapter three explores singular instances of how seven- and eight-year-old children in four schools negotiate the paradoxes and injustices of schooling and, particularly, first communion preparation in a Catholic-dominated school system and consumerist world. The analysis deepens here, as I explore more wide-ranging, unexpected and messy empirical data, with a wider range of children, regarding their encounters with a variety of places, people and objects that are significant to them. This includes schools, churches and significant family events. The chapter shows how children's encounters with people and with material culture (religious icons, mass consumer items, sacred and non-sacred places) complicate prevailing, market-ready categories of religious, spiritual and non-religious child and adult experience.

Through the themes of 'experiencing transcendence' 'watching/being watched' and 'classed, gendered and (a) sexual bodies', I argue that children's encounters with the world involve multiple ways of experiencing joy and belonging, and confronting exclusion and pain. Rather than reproducing societal norms and progressing/failing to progress through a linear series of moral developmental stages, children find various ways of negotiating the differences, conflicts and ambiguities that are present both within and across religious and secular settings. In negotiating school publics and their wider worlds, the plural child does not simply grow 'up' from blank-innocence to all-knowingness. They grow 'sideways', finding creative ways of negotiating their own differences, knowns and unknowns within and beyond generational stages and adults' religious/ secular representation of the world. The data generated with children raised as many, if not more, questions about modes of ethical accountability towards one another as research with adults did. Deep engagement with plurality then, must not simply acknowledge that children make meaning from the world: it must engage children's sideways growth as a way of understanding the paradoxes and challenging the injustices of secular–religious relations in schools.

Chapter four: What matters? The plural child and unequal childhoods

Chapter four examines children's encounters with the world further by focusing more directly on their capacities to deeply engage with plurality, and to act as ethical citizens in and across religious and secular school cultures. Following on from chapter three, I more closely examine children's ethics and forms of citizenship from a critical postsecular perspective. Rather than rely entirely on a pre-defined worldview (rights, reason, science, religion, etc.) to define what a good or bad childhood involves, I examine how children's encounters – largely through the worlds they imagine – may open up ethical relations with multiple ideas, bodies, places, locations and forms of belonging, offering creative, relational ways of being in the world. I also examine how these encounters may close down ethical relations or enact repetition of the same moral codes.

Chapter four examines children's responses to and engagement with a variety of moral issues across multiple geographical scales – specifically materialism, poverty, moral judgement, life and death. The chapter thus demonstrates how children's capacities to act ethically in relation to others are shaped by particular advantages and injustices they experience, and events and phenomena on much broader geographical scales. As the Irish state seeks to implement a national Education for Ethics and Religious Beliefs curriculum, it is argued that meaningful engagement of children's ethics, citizenship and social change must be rooted in multiple and mobile explorations of how place, identity and belonging are felt, defined, imagined and contested in childhood and adulthood.

Chapter five: Remembering childhood, engaging ghosts, imagining school futures

Imaginings of childhood and schooling past, present and future are always plural, making both the remembering and desiring of particular forms of childhood and school inherently ethico-political pursuits. Debates on school provision in Ireland and elsewhere have largely failed to directly engage the role of collective memory and imagination in shaping secular–religious relations and worldviews. Chapter five thus examines the significance of childhood memories, and imaginings of the future, to adults' contemporary worldviews. This analysis is based on interviews, not just with school staff members and parents, but also with older members of the same school localities. As the data analysis here shows, historically collectivist, Catholic views on childhood were frequently reframed by participants in secular–neoliberal terms. Here, favouring 'choice' of worldview, and working on oneself to pursue that worldview, was prioritised. Adults' imaginings of children as growing to choose their worldviews certainly challenges historic Catholic orthodoxy and the pain inflicted on children, amongst many, in that orthodoxy. At the same time, by not acknowledging the exclusion, pain, joy and inclusion that various children are subject to in the present, individualist choice imaginaries also align with white, settled, middle-class adult Catholic (school) majoritarianism. I contend that deep confrontation with the positive and problematic solidarities inherent in majority collective memory need to be seriously considered and broadened as part of public and political discourse which ethically reimagines schooling and childhood in Ireland's present and future.

Chapter six: Building affirmative, unchosen school publics

To quote Braidotti again, the postsecular condition is 'diverse, multicultural, and internally differentiated'.[72] The final chapter draws conclusions about two key aspects of childhood, religion and school injustice, in the context of neoliberal education policy enactments and Catholic school majoritarianism in Ireland. The first relates to the issue of privatisation of schooling, and school patronage in an increasingly marketised education policy context. The second relates to the everyday experiences of children as they move through school and encounter the world. I make the case for supporting education and social movements that build affirmative, unchosen postsecular school publics, which engage children as plural entities, both individually and collectively. Perhaps counterintuitively, the notion of 'unchosen' school publics speaks to developing particular kinds of creative, postsecular freedom, that is situated in our obligations to known and unknown, human and non-human others. The process of developing these publics already happens in multiple ways, at multiple speeds, and does not negate the need for private or faith-forming schools. From a critical postsecular perspective, there is no neatly secular, uniform school landscape on the horizon. Rather, there are multiple education cultures and policy enactments that are more or less emancipatory, and more or less capable of deep, sincere engagement with the plurality of just and unjust past, present and future childhoods and schools.

1

Understanding Worldviews and Placing 'Irish' Childhoods and Schools

Introduction

This chapter examines four overlapping themes. It (a) defines my use of the term 'religious, spiritual and non-religious worldviews', (b) challenges understandings of children as innocent vessels of societal 'reproduction' and considers the ethical possibilities of children and adults 'growing sideways', (c) examines colonial and neoliberal geographies of schooling in Ireland, and (d) summarises some critical postsecular principles for deep political engagement with plurality in education. I contend that all four overlapping themes need to be considered to meaningfully engage and expand debates regarding childhood, religion and schooling in Ireland and internationally.

The first section elaborates on the concept of worldviews, as a way of broadly referring to the plurality of children's and adults' organised and personal, religious, spiritual and non-religious affiliations, beliefs, behaviours, practices and experiences. I present these affiliations, behaviours, etc., not as the unique possessions of individuals or groups, but as diverse processes of encounter. The second section, on 'growing sideways', discusses how adults and children may relate to each other in multiple ways, experiencing joy, pain and pleasure outside of modernity's idealisation of children's preciousness and innocence. It considers that in order for deep engagement of plurality to happen in schools, we need to meaningfully engage both children's and adults' interdependent, plural encounters with the world past, present and future, and the multiple, dynamic ways they experience joy and pleasure, and confront suffering and pain.

The third section provides an analysis of the politics of place, and the scales through which the politics of 'Irish' childhoods, religion and schooling plays out. Understandings of geography (place and scale) and history are vital to deep engagement with plurality. This is because a possessive, ahistorical understanding of place encourages the idea that the culture/worldview/ethnic group that is dominant in a given location should be supported above others. As Connolly argues, deeply committed pluralists prize cultural difference amongst all other things and are prepared to support others in ways that transcend static scales and presumed commonalities of the family, neighbourhood, nation and humanity to support, for example, local and transnational queer religiosities.[1] Deeply committed pluralists engage with diverse histories and, as with this book, diverse histories of Irishness and childhood. The final section summarises the book's overarching principles regarding deep engagement with plurality for public education.

Religious, Spiritual and Non-Religious Worldviews in a Postsecular World

The category of religion has been argued by many academics to have particular features. This includes origins and founder-leaders, key writings and scriptures, a predicament (that is, a serious condition which humanity must escape, such as ignorance), lifestyles, spiritual practices, societal issues, organisation and an ultimate goal.[2] Certainly, worldviews such as nationalism, neoliberalism, rationalism and human rights also have various origins, founder-leaders, key writings and diverse strands. However, religion is often considered unique because of its articulation of goals and relationships that are *transcendent*, or higher than those of the *immanent* or present world. Tweed also argues that adherents to religion 'appeal not only to their own powers but to supra-human (that is, non-human) forces, which can be imagined in varied ways, as they try to intensify joy and confront suffering'.[3]

However, any attempt to present a single or universal definition of religion is loaded with problems and power struggles. As Talal Asad has shown, 'religion' itself is a construct that became globalised through European colonialism.[4] Churches alone did not manufacture the concept of religion. Rather, it emerged as part of the development of modern, secular, colonial–capitalist state authority. A common, oversimplified understanding of secularisation is that it involved religious authority and governance becoming defined as different from, or even opposite to, secular democratic authority and governance. But of course, Irish history alone shows how secular state authority and religious (Catholic) authority can be deeply intertwined. Indeed, there are varying degrees of entanglement between

37

the state as the political model of secularism, and Christian approaches to religion. As the reference to Saba Mahmood's work in the Introduction alluded to, embedded in colonial forms of governance was the Christian (Protestant)-centred ideal that religion involves abstract *beliefs*, that is, thoughts and texts concerned with a reality higher than human incarnation.[5] The problem with this Eurocentric and Platonic reduction of religion to reasoned beliefs is that it often fails to take account of an array of feelings of faith – belonging, devotion, significant/sacred objects and practices that are often characteristic of diverse, deep commitments to religion. In other words, an overemphasis on abstract beliefs downgrades or excludes:

- The role that embodied practical knowledge plays in how people relate to the supernatural and/or the present world. Instead of solely viewing religion as involving the conscious, symbolic 'acting out of belief' (for example, through verbal expressions of creed), we must understand its role in repetitively, intergenerationally composing faith and commitment, through feelings of piety, devotion, and/or wisdom and humility.
- Material culture, including the encountering, making, buying and using of human and non-human entities, which include buildings, land, images, statues, clothing, food and arts. Material culture is crucial to living a religious or spiritual (or indeed non-religious) life in a certain body, place and time. We live in a world not just of ideas, but also of colours, sounds and feelings: our own bodies are constantly changing material things. Our senses bring us into encounters with other things – for example, children at first communion encounter the body of Christ through vision, taste and touch rather than through classroom/church preparation alone.[6]

- Deep human relationships to the spirit(s) of non-human natural matter, such as land, rivers and animals. Contempt for indigenous relations to the natural world helped justify settler colonialism and colonial education, for example, in the case of Native American and Aboriginal Australian land and peoples.
- The specific, personal ways in which children make sense of the world in religious, spiritual or other terms, and the affective, non-rational and non-verbal impact of childhood attachments on adults.

In *Formations of the Secular*, Talal Asad argues for an end to the tendency of separating beliefs from 'disciplinary practices, cultural routines and the education of sensory experience'.[7] As we will see in chapters three and four, in a postsecular world, children and adults encounter the world through their senses, in ways that may 'mix the supernatural, God . . . ethical concerns and prayer together with family, commerce, everyday worries, fashion and social relationships'.[8] For this reason, we cannot presume that things made in our consumerist society are automatically irreligious, or that they have 'replaced religion'. For example, Irish Catholic magical–devotional approaches have long viewed certain things (for example, wells, medals, statues) as having special powers. Our everyday encounters also blur neat distinctions between the secular and religious, public and private. At the same time, such blurring can have unjust consequences. For example, in Ireland, Muslims wearing traditional dress are more likely to be subject to racist abuse.[9] O'Mahony also shows that Catholic symbols such as statues of the Virgin Mary are relatively uncontested aspects of public places.[10] As noted in the Introduction, the promulgation of the Virgin Mary was linked to colonialism 'and the compensatory urge to promote an essential Irishness that was purer – in effect whiter – than other European races'.[11]

Defining worldviews?

Van der Kooij et al. define the concept of 'worldview' in simple terms, as a view on life, the world and humanity, and assert 'every religion may be called a "worldview" but not all worldviews are religious'.[12] This is why we may refer not just to religion, but reason, science, and rights (as well as nationalism, neoliberalism, etc.) as providing the orienting framework for different worldviews. Van der Kooij et al. also distinguish between organised and personal worldviews. Organised worldviews develop over time as an established system with certain sources, traditions, rituals and ideals. Organised worldviews involve existential questions that address matters of ultimate concern (for example, that death is/is not the end of one's existence). They aim to practically influence one's thinking and acting by prescribing answers to existential questions. They involve moral commitments, such as the Buddhist intention to abstain from cruelty and harming others, or the humanist pledge that all people are created equal. Finally, organised worldviews aim to provide meaning in life (for example, reaching Paradise after death) and underline the meaning of other aspects of life (for example, the importance of family). Interestingly, Van der Kooij et al. fail to note that the distinction between 'political' and 'religious' worldviews is blurred – as seen for example, in anti-LGBT+ religious organisations, left-wing liberation theologies, and alt-right atheist movements. They also fail to explore how worldviews involve emotional intensities, connections, and detachments or disconnections, and offer capacities to experience joy and pleasure, and confront suffering and pain.

Personal worldviews may be more or less based in an organised worldview, and involve all of the aforementioned, interacting (existential, practical, moral and meaning) elements of organised worldviews. However, personal worldviews may not be entirely defined, may be morally indifferent (for example, in cases where perceived beauty is privileged over all other concerns), and may draw on multiple sources of knowledge and experience. Beyond dichotomies of organised and personal worldviews, we know that boundaries between religious and non-religious heritage, feeling, affiliation and commitment are also often quite blurred. The terms 'religious', 'spiritual' and 'non-religious' are contested, for various reasons.[13]

For the purposes of identifying the primary orientation of children and parents, this book distinguishes in broad strokes between religious, spiritual and non-religious worldviews. I describe atheist and humanist orientations as 'non-religious', a category which many (particularly younger generations) may identify with, but which is admittedly contested in terms of being defined in deficit relationship to religion. Modern atheist movements, while diverse, are also not typically defined as belief systems or worldviews, in the sense that they are technically against doctrine and prescription. Secular humanism may be more clearly regarded as a worldview premised on reason, ethics and natural laws.[14] Yet some argue that 'new atheist' movements, which have sought to enter public debate to counter religious worldviews, and associated atheist groups who wish to counter literature or celebrations (for example, Darwin Day), also constitute a specific atheist worldview.

As alluded to above, children's and adults' worldviews and experiences often blur the lines of that which may be categorised as religious, spiritual or non-religious. Indeed, the majority of participants' narratives in this book reflect a large degree of deinstitutionalised, spiritual and/or cultural Christianity evident in recent studies of young people and adults.[15] Religious, spiritual and non-religious worldviews are also mediated by classed, racialised, gendered and generational social status, and conservative, liberal and radical politics. This book focuses to a large degree on children and adults' personal worldviews, but, more specifically, on children's and adults' encounters with the world. In other words, I examine how multiple encounters with others, memories, consumer and religious objects influence our capacity to act, think, feel and make sense of the world. Through empirical analysis in chapters two to five, I unpack dynamic, multiple experiences of joy, pain, innocence, knowing, independence and dependence, identification, social recognition and reproduction created through children's and adults' encounters with the world. The rest of this chapter places these experiences in historical and geographic context.

Growing Sideways around Childhood 'Preciousness': Engaging Joy and Suffering

As Erica Burman has outlined, historic and current concerns for colonial/global development and child moral development are entirely entangled.[16] In imperial Britain, the nineteenth-century project of mass schooling aimed to discipline child, industrial working-class and colonial populations who were variously racialised as infantile and incapable of self-governance. Rather than use overt violence, the Victorian era sought to ensure they internalised colonial state moral norms. As I argued in

The Politics of Compulsive Education,[17] the Irish became socially white relative to other British colonial subjects partly through the development of mass schooling. This whiteness as it cemented itself in Catholic, Gaelic nationalist terms was and is anti-nomadic and, as such, systemically racist towards Travellers.

While twentieth- and twenty-first-century societies have adopted less crude and coercive techniques to regulate child morality, these techniques remain, but in more subtle, normative ways. As Karen Smith describes, after the First World War, psychological models of childhood that favoured child-centred thought became increasingly popular.[18] The nineteenth-century, overt focus on moral discipline became displaced somewhat by a twentieth-century focus on children's psychological development and attachment. While these models took longer to embed in Ireland, they were part of a western, science-based, economic view that regarded investment in childhood as an investment in the future.

In the US, Viviana Zelizer argues that the move from child labour to investing in children and delaying their full public participation was part of the sacralisation of childhood, where children largely became valued emotionally or sentimentally.[19] But the contemporary centring of children as precious yet participating appropriately in society – and the desire to view the wellbeing of the child in universally agreed terms – has paradoxical consequences. The value of children, as Dympna Devine shows, is distributed and recognised differently depending on their membership of particular, hierarchised social groups (migrants, citizens, etc.).[20] Contemporary western societies focus attention on the assumed needs and norms of an idealised white, middle-class child, using a postmodern blend of Victorian moral discipline, post-war psychological development, and more contemporary participation ideas, but they continue to minimise or individualise diverse children's fears, joys, sufferings, pleasures and pain.

Van Krieken[21] argues that the rendering of children and childhood as precious is linked to modern society's desire to reproduce itself. Here, adult visions of 'the future' are effectively pinned to children. Reproductive desires – which we likely all experience – need to be analysed, because of their association with heterosexual and human-centred understandings of history, and their tendency to place child-rearing responsibility on the shoulders of individual adults, parents and families.[22] Reproductive desires, as Seán Henry argues, offer 'an image of the future as that which replicates or repeats that which has come before'.[23] For example, politically conservative communities may not wish to recognise that diverse dynamics of affiliation and meaning always already exist within a worldview for both children and adults. On the other hand, more liberal views that children should grow up to 'choose' a religious or other path, incite us to take individual responsibility for our own worldview, which is captured by the emphasis on becoming 'flexible souls'[24] in a neoliberal world. But what if a child submits to transcendent goals above all other concerns in the present?

Kathryn Bond Stockton's conceptualisation of children 'growing sideways' is key to informing my critical postsecular approach to the plural child and unequal childhoods in this book. Many potentially positive or life-affirming relationships with the world are made unavailable to children, or regarded as problematic for them, for the at-times arbitrary and unjust reason of enforcing and maintaining a veneer of (white, middle-class) childhood innocence, preciousness and 'appropriate'

44

participation. Bond Stockton's work on queer childhoods argues that the twentieth-century efforts to craft childhood as innocent and uncomplicated, and thus to make it distant from adulthood, only made children:

> stranger, more fundamentally foreign to adults . . . Given that children don't know this (complex) child, surely not as we (adults) do, though they move inside it, life inside this (child) membrane is largely available to adults as memory – and so takes us back in circles to fantasies (of our memories) . . . the figure of the child does not fit children – doesn't fit the pleasures and terrors we recall.[25]

It could be argued that adults may be more likely to recognise the complex relationships – the 'pleasures and terrors' – they had with the world as children, but such complex child relationships are only available to adults as fantasy-memories, and indeed adult and child mental and emotional states tend to be significantly different.[26] Adults cannot be 'that child' again. However, as discussed below and in chapter five, their being in the world is certainly moved and shaped by imaginings of that child.

The concept of 'growing sideways' was coined by Bond Stockton to engage the nuances of children's (and adults') feelings, bodies and lives in ever-more complex societies. She argues that sideways growth is 'something that locates energy, pleasure, vitality and (e)motion in the back-and-forth of connections and extensions that are not reproductive'.[27] Emotionally, children often 'approach their destinations, delay; swerve, delay; ride on a metaphor they tend to make material and so imagine relations of their own'.[28] Difficult 'destinations' may include the painful realisation that you are different, in the minority, or the 'other'. For example, in chapter three, I discuss how Cathal, who is non-religious but attending a Catholic school, 'rides on a metaphor' of vampires and aliens to imagine his relationship to the local Catholic Church. This imagining allows him to grow sideways, that is, gives him a certain space for pleasure when he is often painfully cast by the largely privatised patron system as other to his Catholic peers and teachers. The next section also discusses research on how minority religious children grow sideways, having to find unusual spaces to pray as a way to combat the Christian-heritage secular rhythms of their school.

Children's encounters with the world may foster reproductive desires, by remaking personal commitments to an organised worldview. That is not necessarily problematic. These encounters may produce a reorientation towards, or a questioning of, that worldview, or another. Or they may creatively make new, unnamed orientations. Importantly, the focus on these encounters highlights children's worldviews (and worldviews themselves) as being in constant formation and transition. Thus despite the appearance of linearity in growing up, children have, to quote Anna Hickey-Moody,[29] 'zigzagging' encounters with persons, objects, images, ideas and places that may ordinarily be cast as not of their generation, or something they are not capable of. Drawing on Rosi Braidotti's work, growing sideways can be considered an ethical practice, whereby the child increases their 'range and span of interconnections' to human and non-human others through complex and continuous negotiations with them.[30] These ideas underline that, in line with an ethos of deep engagement with plurality and the messiness of everyday life, worldviews are not amenable to final mastery or choice.

Children are not the only ones who grow sideways. Despite being tasked with policing age-appropriate behaviour, affectively speaking, adults never entirely inhabit adult (or child) generational states. Through fantasy and/or memories, adults regularly make dynamic connections to multiple images of childhood. By deliberately or unintentionally engaging images from past and future childhoods, adults uniquely intra-act with a child or childhoods, in ways that can close down or open up new cultural and ethical possibilities. Adult-centred, child-focused societies are haunted by painful and traumatic events; sociologically speaking, this trauma reappears in ways that privileged citizens refuse to recognise, or come to terms with. But engaging societal ghosts and hauntings can be constructive. Avery Gordon refers to ghosts as:

> primarily a symptom of what is missing . . . From a certain vantage point the ghost also simultaneously represents a future possibility, a hope . . . the ghost is alive, so to speak . . . it has designs on us such that we must reckon with it graciously, attempting to offer it a hospitable memory out of a concern for justice.[31]

Adults' images of past and future childhoods in Ireland are important to consider in this book for many reasons, not least the very real spectre of child abuse and child institutionalisation. These ghosts live on in the health, education and employment outcomes for Travellers, in the housing/accommodation crisis, and in the failure of our society to challenge the institutionalisation of asylum-seeker children, young people, adults and families. In this context, we need to think about growing sideways, not as a playful option but as a social justice issue. Growing sideways is something that should and can happen throughout life: we need to make lateral connections between past, present and future experiences and images of childhood, to raise historical consciousness that 'enacts accountability for the transnational places we all inhabit in late post-modernity'.[32]

In a globalised world, places are even more intensely connected and contested, through mass information flows and mass production of consumer items, for example. The imaginings of childhood that these connections and contestations create must engage the complexity of children's and adults' lived realities and multiple forms of citizenship across different kinds of schools. Along with experiences of temporality and generation, we need to examine a range of place- and scale-related themes in order to understand the dynamics through which 'Irish' schools, and childhoods, are formed and negotiated.

'Irish' Schools, Secular/Religious Belonging and Multiple Forms of Citizenship

When geographers talk about place, they are referring not just to a locality, but a sense of place and an experience of locatedness.[33] Prevailing definitions of 'this place' are simultaneously dominant definitions of identity, who belongs, and what counts as acceptable forms of interaction. The question of who belongs in Irish schools is also a question of the kind of child citizens, socio-culturally speaking, the Irish state sets out to make.[34] Questions of belonging and citizenship are political, with both a small and big 'p', and are never simply local or even national in nature. They involve contestations of secular and religious organisations, practices and meanings

48

and the blurring of multiple geographical scales of influence – from the individual body, to global policy borrowing on religious education and school governance. In Ireland, accounting for the complexity and current picture of secular and religious schooling means engaging the histories and geographies of:

- How Catholic dominance in Irish primary schooling has been shaped, through a variety of entities cross-cutting different geographical scales. These include bodies, families, schools, parishes, towns, political parties, colonial and independent states, the global and Irish Catholic Church, national and international media, and global education policy movements.
- How, as O'Mahony argues, Irish primary schools have been crucial to local particular kinds of *place-making*.[35] Schools, as particular kinds of places, are contributing to and adapting understandings of what is secular and religious in those places. They therefore contribute to a changing and messy sense of place and sense of 'us'.
- How what becomes defined as a secular or religious place involves 'more than what occurs in particular buildings' such as schools or churches.[36] Material culture – as referred to earlier – includes human and non-human elements that play a role in the formation of a sense of place and a sense of 'us'. As discussed below, public celebrations of first communion have a significant history in this regard.

Below, I briefly consider the significant historic role of the parish structure, the parish school and public first communion ceremonies in defining that local and national sense of 'us' in Ireland. The shape of secular–religious relations in nineteenth-century Ireland was connected to the larger-scale phenomena of colonial capitalism and civilising processes imported from Europe. Similarly, secular–religious public debates, while often having a well-intentioned liberal basis, are very much subject to neoliberal policy logics that exploit religious/non-religious difference to forge the privatisation and marketisation of schooling, and present societal duty in terms of (unequal) self-reliance and responsibility.

The nineteenth-century intensification of Catholic parishes, schools and first communion

The nineteenth century was a key turning point in a struggle between the British state, Rome, Protestant evangelists and an emergent affluent Catholic class for control of the Irish population and its education. Rome had begun a process of tightening the Catholic hierarchy and liturgical practices from the eighteenth century as it became defensive about the rise of nation-state sovereignty in Europe. This process culminated in the declaration of papal infallibility in 1870, and decrees such as *Quam Singulari* (which reduced the age of first communion to seven) in 1910. The key way that relative uniformity in the practices of Catholic clergy and laity was achieved was through the parish structure. Throughout the nineteenth century, Catholic parishes gradually, and unevenly, became the dominant way not only of defining the boundaries of local community, but of embedding the child's moral discipline. The power base of the Catholic Church developed in parishes, through church building, clerical reform, increased vocations, and entanglements with Gaelic nationalist movements including the Gaelic Athletic Association (GAA). The GAA and Catholic schooling remain two of the most influential institutions in Irish childhoods.

As debates regarding Ireland's nineteenth-century 'Tridentine evolution' or 'devotional revolution' suggest, there were multiple elements that helped the success of parish consolidation and Catholic schooling during that century.[37] Paraphrasing Inglis' analysis,[38] the growth in the institutional Catholic Church:

- Was a consequence of economic, educational and demographic growth after the Penal Laws oppressing Catholic clergy and laity had effectively failed. The Catholic Church and religious orders successfully shaped the national school system into denominational, and sectarian, majority Catholic moral habits of mind and body. Gradually increasing literacy also significantly increased understanding and observation of Catholic doctrine.
- Involved adhering to a sexual morality that prioritised stem family structures, where one son inherits all the land, and avoided the further subdividing of already small farms with lower standards of living.
- Imported manners, civility, morality and piety from the European Catholic Church in a way that fused religious interests (through the modelling and surveillance of the parish priest) and class interests (through the benefit accrued to civilised tenant farmers and to the Church through its massive property portfolio).
- Contributed to the further domestication of girls and the naturalisation of women as mothers and housekeepers, chaste and fertile. Women became spiritual protectors of households, by incorporating religious popular material culture: holy water fonts, pictures of the Sacred Heart of Jesus, etc., and by leading rituals such as the rosary.[39] Women's dependency on the Church as the arbiter of good

51

child-rearing made children 'the link between the moralising forces of the Church and the isolated homes of Ireland'.[40] But as Moira Maguire argues, poor and working-class mothers lived in fear that their children would be taken away 'because endemic poverty made it impossible for them to raise their children according to middle class standards and expectations'.[41]

Regular receipt of the eucharist had become a feature of life for Catholics in Ireland by the end of the nineteenth century, making first communion, for both adult and child communicants, a significant public event and symbol of local and national belonging. Public celebrations of first communion for young people began in France in the late sixteenth century, spreading quickly and helping reinforce the devotional and institutional strength of Catholic communities. The emotive spectacle of young piety affected adults, sustained parish vitality and was intended to underline the importance of the event for the communicants through their lives. McGrail notes that while early public first communion events reinforced young people's 'adherence to the Church and its priorities, this ambition began to be subverted from at least the eighteenth century onwards'.[42] Material culture, defined as 'non-ecclesial elements', were increasingly 'assimilated into the event'. This included a celebratory family meal, which extended the church event, and increased care for communicants' appearance including white dresses for girls. Historic and contemporary concerns over the appearance of children, and particularly girls, at first communion are unpacked further in chapter three.

In the period leading up to the partition of Ireland and southern independence, the Catholic Church successfully defended against the British development of local authority management of primary schools. The mutually reinforcing nature of class interests, religious interests, patriarchal norms, regular adherence to sacraments, and submission to clerical surveillance meant that parishes and the broader Irish Catholic Church maintained a virtual monopoly on independent 'state' schooling, and what constituted a good childhood until the 1960s at the earliest. The official purpose of education was, until then, focused on transcendent goals, that is, preparation for the afterlife. In the context of a largely agrarian, unindustrialised society, social teaching was focused on 'the defence of rural life and Catholic public morality'.[43] Catholic schools were strongly viewed as a local resource for a taken-for-granted community.[44] At primary level, first communion ceremonies continue to be an important ritual part of maintaining this majoritarian sense of 'us' and, as McGrail argues, a 'focus for the structural aspirations of the Catholic Church'.[45]

Twenty-first-century neoliberal secular–religious relations: Performing citizenship(s)

It has been acknowledged for some years that many of those identifying as Catholic in Ireland see themselves as 'belonging to a religious heritage without embodying institutional beliefs and practices' and that they are 'becoming more like their Protestant counterparts' across Europe.[46] A 2018 Pew study found that, in Ireland, 46 per cent of the population identified as non-practising Christians, equalling the Western European median.[47] 34 per cent identified as church-attending Christians, the second highest after Portugal (35 per cent). Pew also found that amongst countries involved, 87 per cent of non-practising Christians were raising their children as Christian.

This rose to 92 per cent in Ireland. School-based rituals such as first communion, then, are clearly not steeped in religious devotion for quite a large section of Ireland's young families. However, sacraments remain important to maintaining a deeply embodied and privileged sense of white, settled, Irish Catholic ethno-religious identity. A 2016 survey by the Irish NGO Equate showed that, of a representative sample of 351 Catholic parents of children of school-going age (3–15 years), 53 per cent stated that they baptised their child for faith/personal belief reasons and 58 per cent stated it was for family tradition reasons. Out of 400 parents, 24 per cent agreed/strongly agreed with the idea that they would not have baptised their child if they didn't need it to gain entry to school; 55 per cent disagreed/strongly disagreed with this idea.[48]

The Irish Catholic Church and its local patrons have repositioned themselves, and been repositioned, as one player amongst others in the now globalised Irish education market. On the face of it, schools across the country have slowly and unevenly been reconstituted as spaces of public education, not least through the sustained involvement of parents, predominantly mothers, in primary-school affairs since the 1970s. Sustained efforts to interrogate the exclusion of minority religious and non-religious children, particularly since the 2012 publication of the *Report of the Advisory Body of Forum on Patronage and Pluralism* (discussed in chapter two), have also been a key factor in Catholic institutional repositioning. Institutional Catholic contributions to public discourse have deployed notions of rights, religion, reason and the market in various, problematic and majoritarian ways.[49] For example, the Catholic Schools Partnership's 2015 publication, *Catholic Primary Schools in a Changing Ireland*, adopted the contradictory rhetoric of defending in-school sacramental preparation as a religious right, while defining inclusion of minority religious and non-religious children largely in terms of 'opt outs'.[50] This publication selectively hailed Catholic school inclusiveness on the basis of social class, disability and Traveller identity, by noting 2012 evidence from the Economic and Social Research Institute (ESRI) that minority faith and multi-denominational schools in Ireland had higher proportions of children from middle-class backgrounds than Catholic schools.[51] Yet ESRI researchers, Darmody et al., state that this is 'not surprising' given the active choices parents make in this regard, as 'in most areas children have to travel further to attend these school types'.[52] Half of children in multi-denominational schools were Catholic, and Catholic schools were predominantly Catholic. However, multi-denominational schools were more likely to have higher proportions of minority ethnic children whose parents were born outside of Ireland. All of this data comes with a health warning: not only is some of it years old, each particular school demographic is different.

The multiplicity of secular–religious meanings in a given school locality, and the related ambiguity of who constitutes the local public/citizenry to be educated, is not unique to Ireland, or the twenty-first century. Citizenship involves a much wider range of phenomena than legal rights and responsibilities and is multi-layered in its articulation of who belongs, who can fully exercise rights, and to whom we have obligations.[53] In a secular English school setting, Hemming[54] analysed how religious citizenship overlapped with ethno-national citizenship. This school implicitly drew upon Christianity, in part, to offer a greater level of rights and belonging to certain students. The right of minority religion and non-religious students to wear particular symbols, eat particular foods, fast, and be withdrawn from particular lessons were respected – but certain restrictions, such as timetable rhythms and health and safety requirements, were premised in legal and disciplinary norms developed in a western Christian model. Children of minority religions found creative ways of contesting or circumventing these constraints – 'growing sideways' and implicitly mediating/contesting their framing as other – by, for example, using the space of a toilet as a temporary, private space to pray. Local student, teacher and parent practices in the school were linked to imaginings of British national identity as being Christian in nature. Thus performances of citizenship, identity and belonging use, traverse, blur and contest the meaning of different geographical scales. The local act of privileging Christian students in the officially secular school is linked to a wider, implicitly Christian imagining of national identity, while the cultivation of furtive, strange places to pray jars with the modernist fantasy of secularism as politically neutral.

It is crucial to remember also, that understandings of child moral agency and participation, while based on principles of democratic communication and negotiation, are commonly exploited by neoliberal values of competition, hyper-rational choice and enterprise. Here, 'in order to manage individual risk . . . child educational subjects . . . are positioned as "autonomous choosers" . . . which serves to problematize young people who do not "choose" appropriately'.[55] In chapter three, I particularly address the classed and racialised charge of Catholic irrationality and failure placed at the feet of working-class and Traveller girls and their families. It is welcome that broad public rejection of arbitrary Catholic school majoritarianism has brought a focus on how deeply held certain

(Catholic) worldviews are. However, this rejection can be used to conflate two issues, namely Catholic school dominance, and the diverse, classed, racialised and gendered material cultural expression that is characteristic of all childhoods and worldviews. This conflation facilitates the public, stigmatising presentation of children as passive or flawed citizens, and adults as either entirely rational or entirely irrational choosers of schools, worldviews and their associated practices.

Echoing existing research in Ireland, chapters two to five will demonstrate how what counts as 'Irish' (national) childhoods and families can be contested – through the shaping and imagining of children and parents as belonging, or belonging less, based on their religious/family heritage, skin colour, or their location within a relatively static rural population versus a more diverse, mobile and urban school population.[56] As addressed in chapter two, woven in here is the role that classed and gendered family mobilities (that is, the movement and containment of families and relationships) play both in how place and belonging are defined, and how ideas, bodies and practices are relatively reproduced, altered or left behind.

Conclusion: Mapping Deep Political Engagement with Plurality

Recalling the discussion of a relatively fluid, contingent ethics of commonality in the Introduction, a key point from the above discussion is that engagement with plurality cannot be based on absolutes of reason, rights, religion, science, or indeed market or nation. Rather, we must pursue an understanding of the plurality of the child and multiple, mobile understandings of how they feel, define, imagine and contest place, identity and belonging. I have already noted a number of key principles of what I regard as deep engagement with plurality from a critical postsecular perspective, but it is useful to summarise these principles here. First, the capacity to engage with the fallibility and contestability of one's own worldview is central to deep engagement with plurality. While I am making the case for supporting the becoming public of schools and the Irish school system, this engagement with fallibility and contestability is possible both in religious and secular schools. As William Connolly puts it, 'you love your creed . . . but you appreciate how it appears opaque and profoundly contestable to many who do not participate in it'.[57] This forms the basis for an agonistic, constructively contested relationship between different worldviews: 'you absorb the agony of having elements of your own faith called into question by others, and you fold agonistic contestation of others into the respect that you convey towards them'.[58]

Worldviews are not abstract bodies of rational thought, where agonistic contestation and creative and imaginative ruptures happen through rational, principled debate and dialogue. Worldviews are always already deeply embodied and often empassioned. Drawing on Connolly's work, Finlayson argues that in any encounter with the Other, intense emotions may be exchanged that cannot be accounted for in advance. To think we can overcome these:

> by some act of rational will (as if it were entirely separate from our visceral emotional experience) is to misunderstand the nature and potential of such encounters, perhaps also to hide from ourselves the existential resentments that cause us to be fearful of our current disposition . . . an

encounter between others might lead not only to a greater understanding of, or appreciation for, what 'is', but to something new that nobody was preparing for.[59]

Thus deep engagement with plurality requires not just openness to fallibility and contestability, but to the unknown: to feelings and experiences that encounters with other humans and non-human material culture may produce. Our worldviews are also shaped by multiple social hierarchies, and the material interests, advantages and disadvantages these hierarchies confer. These hierarchies need to be accounted for, particularly when thinking about the multiply majoritarian nature of the school system and how it benefits white, middle-class, Catholic heritage families in particular. The arbitrariness of Catholic institutional power, and the fact that religious, spiritual and non-religious worldviews are entangled with their material interests, however, does not mean that the pursuit of worldviews is inherently cynical. Drawing on Pellandini-Simányi,[60] religious, spiritual and non-religious worldviews are not linked to material interests because of an intrinsically self-interested human nature, but because of the normative nature of morality itself. Socio-religious norms are double-edged. They imply hierarchies of who and what is valued in a given field, and yet our affiliation with them also offers us recognisability as persons in such fields.[61]

The experience of agonistic relations with those categorised as different, and the 'element of rupture or mystery already simmering' in one's own worldview, can be used to foster deep engagement with plurality or 'marshal its repression'.[62] It is important in the Irish context that we distinguish between responses to changes within Catholicism in Ireland: those which enable a destructive holding to arbitrary Catholic majoritarianism in schooling, and those that offer creative ways of engaging with

59

others within and outside of institutional Catholicism. Examples of creativity may include the different ways children from different social class groups practice their religiosity through specific forms of material culture (including candles and communion dresses – see the discussion of Lily in chapter three).

Alexander offers a vision for liberal Jewish faith schooling that prioritises transcendence, but not in the religious sense (where a reality beyond the present/immanent world is *the* ultimate good). He argues it is important to be able to transcend 'the consciousness and history' of a particular faith community, 'encouraging us to recall that every point of view is fallible'.[63] However, given the tendency of neoliberal societies to exploit images of diversity, it is important that a paternalistic liberalism, where 'we' 'accommodate' and 'tolerate' the Other, does not underpin admissions of fallibility and contestability. Rather, one's worldview must always already be recognised as percolating with plurality that is to some extent uncategorisable and possibly felt, rather than articulated. For example, as Seán Henry notes, efforts to engage with the radically new must be capable of resisting the exclusion of uncategorisable, queer bodies and perspectives in a faith school context. This is an *educational* effort, as it takes seriously:

> the educational imperative of encountering others with whom we relate, in all their bodily specificity and unknowability . . . those whose identities deviate from orthodox . . . doctrine (including, for instance, those that identify as queer) come to be seen as themselves constitutive of, and contributive to, the life of the school, and not as . . . deviations from the norm that are to be negotiated with or overcome.[64]

Another core example of the uncategorisable is that of childhood and children themselves: children's early encounters with worldviews are perhaps more explicitly – but not uniquely – sensory, pre-verbal and experimental than those of adults. Deep engagement with plurality means deep engagement with the diversity and relative ambiguity of affiliations, beliefs, practices, belongings, and experiences of *children* within and outside of particular worldviews. This engagement should not rely entirely on reproductive desires, which appear to privilege children's lives above adults but in reality disengage the nuances of their lived experience. Rather it involves growing sideways: engaging the dynamic, multiple experiences of pleasure, pain, indulgence, sacrifice, piety, apathy, joy, sadness, uncertainty, identification and the desire for social recognition and reproduction created through children's and adults' encounters in a decidedly non-rational world and non-linear life-course. Ultimately, the analysis of lived experience in this book, despite focusing on white, settled, Irish Catholic origins to a large extent, is aimed at cultivating an understanding of the plural affiliations and practices internal to all worldviews.[65] Children are regarded as constituting diverse, interdependent minorities within and between worldviews, where the religious/ non-religious boundaries of worldviews themselves are always blurred and subject to negotiation and contestation.

Recognising that different worldviews percolate with plurality means that no worldview can claim itself to have a monolithic majority. This recognition poses a challenge to the leadership of school patrons and organised (particularly societal, majority) worldviews. The challenge is to admit that doubt, mystery and diversity punctuate both religious and non-religious worldviews, and to develop a culture of presumptive generosity and ethical accountability towards others. However, the prizing of cultural diversity and presumptive generosity within and across worldviews does have limits. The liberal stance that 'every view is fallible' itself needs to be contested when it comes to questions of objective social injustice. This is relevant, given the generosity of the Irish Forum on Patronage to all patrons' interests, and the fact that Catholic interests far outweighed all others (see chapter two). It is also particularly relevant in a global climate where the emboldening of far-right-wing, racist, fascist and homophobic sentiment, right-wing anti-Traveller and anti-asylum-seeker attitudes in Ireland and ongoing settler–colonial conditions in states such as Israel are pandered to through distorted and relativist notions of 'balance' and 'respecting all views'. As my discussion of the ghosts of colonialism and institutionalisation of children indicates, engagement with plurality requires us to:

> embrace certain things in this particular place, to be indifferent to some, to be wary of others, and to fight militantly against the continuation of yet others . . . pluralists set limits to tolerance to ensure that an exclusionary . . . movement does not take over an entire regime.[66]

Furthermore, it is crucial to not assume that all individuals and groups can be equally generous in engaging with others. As Moya Lloyd asks: 'what happens to those bodies and subjects for whom generosity is difficult, if not impossible?' She argues that 'rather than generosity being a precondition for democratic engagement for such persons, it may be precisely resentment that enables them to act; resentment at being, what Judith Butler calls, "unintelligible"'.[67] Historically, non-conforming women and mixed-race, minority religious and non-religious children have been unintelligible (that is, not recognisable) as ethical beings in Catholic and state institutions. The social movements these injustices and their ghosts have generated in response – such as Justice of Magdalenes, Mixed Race Ireland, Movement of Asylum Seekers in Ireland and Education Equality – are examples of how passion and resentment have productively, if not always unproblematically, created claims for citizenship and belonging, and necessarily forced engagement with plurality.

While not referencing the postsecular predicament explicitly, Alexander provides a useful grounding of, and guiding principles for, these complexities in the context of schooling. He argues for a space for both common and faith schools, but also that we need to be able to distinguish between orientations that promote a way of being for common life across difference and apparently incommensurable cultures and those that do not. In this regard, he distinguishes between moral/ethical and amoral/non-ethical ideologies (or worldviews). Moral/ethical worldviews are capable of engaging human freedom, intelligence and fallibility – concepts that are 'not morally neutral, but . . . do allow for a wide degree of pluralism within reasonable limits'.[68] Amoral/non-ethical worldviews believe they have the whole truth and deny human freedom, intelligence and fallibility. I contend that, in the context of 'nomadic ethics' discussed in chapter four, values of presumptive generosity, agonistic openness to fallibility and contestability of one's worldview, engagement of the uncategorisable (potentially including children's experiences and adults' memories), engagement of the centrality of material culture to all worldviews, intolerance of fascist, racist, sexist, ageist and other unjust ideologies and practices, acknowledgement of legitimate resentment, and the challenging of majoritarianism and multiple related injustices support deep engagement with plurality and, as such, ethical accountability towards known and unknown others. The challenges and possibilities that these commitments raise will be explored further throughout the forthcoming chapters.

2

Contested, Unchosen School Publics: Parents Negotiating School 'Choice'

Introduction

Lynch and Moran argue that Ireland's second-level school system has been effectively marketised historically, through the principle of freedom of religious conscience in where one sends one's child(ren) to school.[1] The marketisation of education policy discourse and school provision at primary level has taken on a more explicit form in recent years. Education policy discourse has drawn on contradictory values and ideas – including austerity, diversity, self-reliant choice and rights – translating and making sense of them at local level for the purposes of making patrons compete for parental attention.[2]

This chapter poses the question of what a 'secular education system' can mean in Ireland and elsewhere, given this complex and unjust policy landscape. I contend that any discussion of secular–religious relations in education must confront the possibilities and limits of defining the 'public to be educated' given three key challenges:

1. When it comes to education governance, absolute religious or non-religious neutrality and universally understood common ground is a myth, and distinctions between public and private space often break down.
2. Nation-state sovereign governance of religious and non-religious expression is vexed. This is in part due to supra-national governance, and the diversity of local publics. It is also vexed because reliance on state policy to define 'the public' may hide the symbolic violence enacted through market-led policies.
3. We need to consider what can positively emerge from the failure of public education to be based on neutral grounds and universally understood values. Importantly, the values and ideas expressed in global and Irish education policy discourse regarding the public governance of schooling (for example, austerity, rights, diversity, choice) are not simply abstract notions that have fixed, universally agreed meaning. In fact neoliberal policy enactments successfully merge often such contradictory values and ideas in order to legitimise and deepen the self-interested privatisation and marketisation of schooling.

This chapter demonstrates the need for policy discourse in Ireland to adopt an understanding of school localities as contested, unchosen publics and to continuously, constructively engage agonistic/contested relationships between different populations and worldviews, rather than forcing competition between school patrons for parents' attention and cultivating 'active' choosers. The chapter analyses interviews with parents from the four primary-school localities, which include nine schools in total, located in different parts of Ireland. It examines how parents encounter, shape and become shaped by multiple, sometimes contradictory, policy values and ideas such as austerity, choice, diversity and rights.

The data in this chapter builds on previous research conducted by Dympna Devine and Smyth et al., respectively, on diverse parents' relationships to school type in Ireland.[3] Two key themes arose from the parent interview data in this study in relation to understanding schools as contested, unchosen publics. These were (1) how racialised, classed and gendered dynamics of family mobility shape the rural and urban, messy formation of local school publics and secular–religious relations and (2) the need to distinguish between doubt and diversity *within* Catholic family traditions, and an arbitrary white, middle-class Catholic majoritarianism seen in many parents' 'default' preference for Catholic schools. Interviews demonstrate that the definition of 'us' as a school community, and subsequent engagement with plurality across localities, is consciously and unconsciously contested, place specific and entangled with wider geographical scales (for example, the nation, the globe). In other words, family–school dynamics are locally unique but entirely connected into the national and global reshaping of secular–religious governance, identity, citizenship and belonging. Before getting to this data, I unpack the arguments stated at the beginning of the chapter.

Beyond Universal Common Ground: Letting the Market Take Care of it?

This book's critical postsecular perspective explicitly engages with Alexander's direct point that 'there are no neutral grounds, rational or otherwise, upon which to base the commonality of schooling'.[4] It is commonly recognised in public discourse that confessional schools present partisan worldviews. But it is important to recognise that rationalist approaches to learning about and from religion that are characteristic of public-school movements are also not neutral. European policy discourse on religious education (RE) in public schools, such as the *Toledo Guiding Principles*, has favoured education about religion, underpinned by a human rights framework, for some time.[5] As discussed below, this approach has become increasingly popular in Ireland, as indicated by the growth of the Educate Together equality-based school movement, which now is the (private) patron of around 100 Irish primary schools. Of course, education about religions, beliefs and ethics reduces intolerance and increases mutual understanding, and it needs deep support in Ireland and beyond.[6] But alongside the critique of rights as a non-neutral basis for education (discussed in the Introduction), rationalist approaches to education about religions, beliefs and ethics are not a panacea. It cannot be assumed that secular schools offering a critical rationalist engagement of worldviews provide a universal, neutral basis for engagement with plurality. Alexander contends that critical rationalism:

> was thought to provide non arbitrary, relevant criteria for choosing between competing ideologies . . . it turns out that reasons cannot be justified as the non arbitrary

grounds for choosing among ideologies in a way that does not assume what it sets out to prove, since such a justification would itself require a reason.[7]

In order to prove its superiority to, for example, religiosity as a neutral common ground, critical rationalism must assume what it sets out to prove, using its own criteria (of rational proof) to do so. Critical rationalism may also neglect the role that emotions play in encounters with different others. Additionally, at European level, Gearon argues that civil religious education public discourse shows minimal tolerance for social justice theologies, and that public discourse on RE reproduces an assumed link between religiosity, conflict and security risks.[8]

These critiques do not mean that movements for public and non-confessional approaches to religious and ethical education should be abandoned. Rather, it means that they are imperfect and should be engaged in creative ways. I use the term 'contested' when referring to secular–religious school publics and associated forms of RE, but, as referenced in the Introduction, this term does not refer to a negative, wholly oppositional set of identities between families and schools. In fact, contestation can create feelings and experiences of commonality. It is important to recognise that religious and common schools, as Hemming relates, typically share 'an appreciation of nature, awe, wonder and human relationships . . . right and wrong, tolerance, respect, caring and honesty . . . (and) the personal development of children.[9] Hemming also notes that schools are not limited to abstract values – they cultivate practices and identities – and that we need to recognise in particular how Christian religious heritage permeates common school settings.

Hemming emphasises a postsecular ethic focused on 'religious and secular interests coming together for the common good' and, despite difficulties, examining the 'high level of congruence that can exist between religious and secular perspectives'.[10] This is important. But, as discussed below in relation to the differential mobilities and experiences of families, my critical postsecular perspective more directly highlights the need for an understanding that school publics are unchosen and traversed by contingent, unequal (classed, racialised, gendered), agonistic relations between people and communities that entirely mediate/underpin the expression of religious, spiritual and non-religious worldviews through schools. For example, a 2016 parent survey by the NGO Equate found that, in order, location, reputation, ethos and availability of school places available were the most important factors in considering what school to send one's eldest child to.[11] At least the first two of these factors can be considered to be explicitly classed and racialised when we consider which families have greatest access to the 'best' neighbourhoods and 'most reputable' schools.

It is vital, then, to think constructively beyond the failure of public education to find neutral, universal ground. I argue that we must think of school localities as complex, multi-layered publics involving encounters between bodies, buildings and places that are related to contestations of religious and secular meaning on a variety of geographical scales. Furthermore, 'secular' education policies need to be analysed in terms of how they are enacted in neoliberal ways, how they help make certain kinds of self-interested majoritarian school publics, and how such enactments contribute to unjust national and global political trends. Unfortunately, public policy and law-makers tend to 'let the market take care of it'.

The global (re)turn to school marketisation: Parents and patrons under pressure

Internationally, state education policy makers have turned, or returned, to the privatisation and marketisation of schooling in order to diversify available school types according to parents' religious, cultural, or linguistic concerns for their children's education.[12] Religious and non-religious organisations have little option but to be part of, and to be defined by, the technically secular public sphere on marketised, individualist terms, where their role in the business of education involves appealing to worldly rather than transcendent goals.[13] The ways in which policies of secular/religious school community recognition become enacted involve a range of interacting forces operating through multiple geographical scales. These include historic state–religion partnerships, public planning regulations, communications media, transnational non/religious civil society organisations, and imaginings of local and national identity.[14] The trans-scalar nature of these forces suggests the sovereign religious neutrality of the nation-state to be vexed, to say the least.

Certainly, the normalisation of market choice policies across countries can offer certain opportunities for collective, alternative religious, ethnic or equality-based school movements that create collective resistances to exclusionary and/or majoritarian schooling.[15] But examples of the hidden inequalities that develop or are sustained in privatised and marketised school policy enactments abound. For example, Gulson and Webb examine attempts to found private Islamic schools to offer greater choice to Muslim families in Sydney.[16] They outline histories of racialised opposition to Islamic private school plans, which

71

draw on elements such as religiously/racially 'neutral' local government planning concerns over traffic flow and land use, and media-based, openly racist fears of Muslim incompatibility with local community and/or Australia's purportedly Christian heritage. Elsewhere, the differential resources available to religious organisations historically associated with states offer certain organisations an advantage in branding themselves favourably, as seen in research on Catholic schools in certain US and Australian states.[17]

Calls for the diversification or secularisation of the Irish primary-school sector have not come from movements like Educate Together alone, although Educate Together has pioneered 'equality-based' schooling. Some Catholic leaders and advocates, including Dublin Archbishop Diarmuid Martin, have also led these calls. Since 2011, two right-wing-led government coalitions have been the first to explicitly examine the issue of non/religious recognition in Irish primary schooling. They framed the question not in terms of public education as such, but in terms of lack of school diversity and parental choice. A statutory Forum on Patronage and Pluralism in the Primary Sector (hereafter termed 'the Forum') was established very quickly after as then Minister Ruairí Quinn took over, after the previous cabinet collapsed in economic and political chaos. The Forum was a significant event in the history of Irish education, as it made the configuration of patronage (but not the idea of patronage) an issue of formal public deliberation. The Forum Advisory Group worked in a sincere and efficient manner to review constitutional, legal and scholarly texts, and took submissions and feedback from hundreds of parties, including eighty-one children. But in a context of radical budgetary austerity, the Forum's remit was to be 'cost-neutral'.

This meant the radical revisioning of the primary-school system, for example, dismantling state-funded school patronage from the outset, was disavowed. The idea of cost-neutrality was critiqued by the Forum Advisory Group's 2012 report, and the idea of funding the localised transfer of Catholic schools to other patrons in targeted areas was recommended.[18] The report recommended the surveying of pre-school parents' preference of school type to this end. Another key recommendation was to develop a national Education about Religion and Beliefs (ERB) and ethics curriculum (discussed in chapter six).

The local surveying process expressly avoided facilitating public meetings on the transfer of patronage. This was understandable in certain respects, given the intensity of focus that would be placed on particular school areas tipped for transfer/patron divestment. But it indicated that the 'consultation' that could happen remained under the long shadow cast by Catholic trusteeship of most schools, and competition with thirteen other patrons for those schools. The development of a state New Schools Establishment Group, while positive in comparison to the haphazard approach taken previously, meant that school quasi-publics were conflated with 'a market for the free exchange of goods', formed through 'dialogue between those groups with dominance in that market'.[19] By November 2015, Chair of the Advisory Group, Professor John Coolahan (now deceased), publicly stated his disappointment that, by that time, 'local (Catholic) patrons and politicians stayed at a distance when they should have done more to encourage confidence'.[20] This was in spite of the spirit of 'generosity' with which the Forum operated. By January 2017, only a handful of primary-school buildings no longer in active use had been divested of Catholic patronage.

Thus in 2017, Minister for Education and Skills, Richard Bruton, announced that the government wished to reach a target of 400 non- and multi-denominational primary and post-primary schools by 2030 – around 10 per cent of all state-funded schools by current figures. This plan involved new school builds, divesting schools by leasing them from Catholic patrons and the surveying of parental preferences by local Education and Training Boards (ETBs). ETBs are patrons of self-described multi-denominational, equality-based Community National Schools. Thus, the Minister's plan was framed as being in the public (state, taxpayer) interest. This was somewhat cynical, given the leading role that Educate Together and other related movements have had in changing education policy discourse. Indeed, Educate Together was forced to argue about lack of transparency in a way that implicitly positioned them as a disgruntled competitor to ETB schools.[21]

Three main effects have emerged from recent Irish governments' increased efforts to define the education public in marketised terms. First, post-Forum policy has minimally engaged the national question of existing (largely Catholic) schools and set patron bodies further against each other, despite some strategic (for example, Catholic–ETB) alliances. It has encouraged parents to 'recreate' the school system through local choice levers and, in the meantime, encouraged them to send children to the 'school of their choice'. Certainly, due to pressure from campaign groups such as Equality in Education and Equate, the Education (Admissions to Schools) Act 2018 has brought some positive change, in terms of supporting access to one's local school. Ending the 'baptism barrier', which has historically legally entitled oversubscribed Catholic schools to give enrolment priority to Catholic children, was an important precedent. But this barrier was an issue in around 20 per cent of schools, largely in urban settings. These national policy measures have been focused primarily on cultivating actively choosing parents, and tweaking state-funded patronage, rather than persistently challenging its colonial development and its underfunded, effectively privatised, quasi-public existence.

Second, the financialised logic of post-austerity neoliberalism requires a return on investment from local service providers as what McGimpsey calls 'a form of futures market'.[22] This is discernible in the DES' piecemeal approval of alternative school patrons, which 'strengthen and expand diversity in the area served by the school'.[23] Modest secular/religious school diversity is 'vampirised' here as a potential that is latent for future commodification, and not as an intrinsic feature of Irish society in itself. This point echoes Audrey Bryan's critique of the intercultural diversity management paradigm present in recent Irish education policy history.[24] Indeed, engagement with diversity was articulated in the data below, at times as a commodity for the majority, rather than as something inherent to life, and requiring solidarity. Third, as discussed throughout the book, an intensified focus on parents' and children's rights to the school of their choice has also led to somewhat understandable but at times classed, racialised and gendered critiques of certain Catholic families' 'inauthentic' religiosity. Overall then, education policy enactments continue to facilitate piecemeal chess-games, around a very specific kind of secular, consumer freedom in schools, that might erode Catholic school management over a very long period, but which ultimately distracts from deep political engagement with questions of contested, unchosen publics, and the shaping of social and cultural capitals intergenerationally.

75

Schools involved in the fieldwork

The forthcoming sections examine the multi-layered ways in which contested and overlapping family interests play out across four school localities. They demonstrate the various, at times contradictory, values and views of parents as they negotiate a school sector that increasingly valorises a middle-class-advantaging bias towards active parent choice, (unequal) individual responsibility and self-interest, above all other principles. Some excerpts from school principals are also provided to offer context on different school localities. The schools discussed in the analysis are described in table 2.1 below, in order to provide some context for understanding the school localities in this chapter and others.

Schools in different parts of the country participated. Given the intimate size of the Irish primary sector, I have not identified the regional location of each school in order to minimise the risks of each school and participant being identifiable.[25] Parents were interviewed individually, in pairs and in focus groups. The majority of the research was conducted between January and April 2013, when the country was in the grip of government austerity budget cuts. Asterisks are placed beside the four schools where we conducted in-depth participatory research with children (discussed in chapters three and four) and where we conducted more in-depth individual/pair parent interviews.

Table 2.1. Schools that took part in the study

Fairglen Catholic School*	Socio-economically mixed, predominantly white, settled, Irish, rural, long established
Raven Hill Educate Together School*	Disadvantaged, predominantly minority ethnicities, city suburb, recently established
St Michael's Catholic School	Socio-economically mixed, ethnically mixed, city suburb, recently established
Deansfort Educate Together School	Middle-class, predominantly white, settled, Irish, city suburb, recently established
St Brendan's Catholic School	Socio-economically mixed, ethnically mixed, city suburb, long established
Inis Educate Together School	Disadvantaged, ethnically mixed, city suburb, recently established
Scoil Cholmcille Catholic School*	Socio-economically mixed, predominantly white, settled, Irish, town, long established
Grange Church of Ireland[26] School	Socio-economically mixed, ethnically mixed, town, long established
St Gerard's Catholic School*	Disadvantaged, predominantly white, settled, Irish, city, long established

As noted at the beginning of the chapter, two themes emerged as important in terms of understanding complex, unequal school publics: *mobilities* and *majoritarianism*.

Mobilities and Immobilities

The concept of mobilities refers to relative social, spatial, collective and individual movement and exchange of bodies, objects, media (for example, newspapers), affects and ideas, the restriction of that movement and exchange, and the relationships, trajectories and meanings that form, change and end through such processes.[27] Examples of mobility practices generated through families include the school run, moving house, and holidays – all of which involve collective and individual negotiation of social status (class, race, gender, age) and social space. School uniforms are both objects and ideas that shape movement towards particular schools, while immobility may arise from the intangible 'feel' from a certain building or interaction.

Mobility and immobility processes help make school localities particular kinds of places, and help maintain, reshape or sever socio-religious intergenerational connections. Holdsworth[28] asserts that mobilities associated with sustaining family life (for example, the school run) are more likely to be engaged by women. Darmody et al.'s report notes that multidenominational schools in Ireland tend to be more middle-class due to parents' greater mobility/active choice. Additionally, they note that levels of parental education have a much stronger effect on school selection than occupation.[29] Both of these dynamics were evident in the suburban data below. Indeed, it was clear in comparing rural, suburban and urban data, and the experiences of diverse parents, that mobility and immobility was important to understanding how they articulated different values and, indeed, hurts as they negotiated school 'choice', or lack thereof.

Fairglen and rural mobilities

Fairglen Catholic School is a multigrade school in a village of over 400 people surrounded by farming hinterland. There was a degree of unemployment in the area, and many who were working commuted to the small city twenty to thirty minutes away. The school is part of a rural parish which has some other Catholic village schools and a parish GAA team. There is also a second- level, interdenominational school nearby, which attracts students from multiple rural areas and markets itself as combining the rural idyll with closeness to the city. The nearest alternative type of primary schools are in the city. Fairglen faced challenges in ensuring it retained teachers due to declining enrolments. Our interview with the principal focused partly on the school's open- day efforts:

Fairglen Principal: We were kind of promoting yesterday that children were important . . . they were the people who lead people around and guided people around and answered questions . . . That they participate very fully, like we have a very wide curriculum and a wide, you know, various activities going on in school like that. We also wanted to promote the atmosphere and the collegiality that's there between staff but also that's there with children . . . Obviously the whole academic area, we wanted to promote that as well . . . and I suppose like the care that we have for children.

The principal also indicated the need to ensure that any reputation that the village had as being 'rough' was challenged.

79

The above partly signals how larger-scale, interacting processes of religious deprivatisation, austerity, urbanisation, marketisation and child citizenship shape a rural school setting. In terms of deprivatisation, this Catholic school is clearly part of a public sphere, as it is focused on the wide national curriculum and developing children as citizens for the present world. However, amidst the 'promotion' of the school (a term I used in the interview), Catholic instruction, culture and an emphasis on the transcendent was not erased, and the term 'parish' was used by most participants to define the locality's boundaries. The school's Catholic ethos was somewhat taken for granted, as there were no alternatives to Catholic schooling in the area – making it unchosen in a very tangible way. While choice of religious or secular school is a moot point in this locality, parents were still encouraged to choose *this* (Catholic) school over others in the area. As such, the making of the school as a place involved a slowly shifting 'bundle' of secular and religious meanings.[30]

The concrete ways the local place, community and belonging were defined and quietly contested became evident in parent interview analysis. Despite living in the area for ten years, Susan defined her family as 'blow-ins', because they were 'non-native' (from the UK) and 'non-Catholic'. Susan was Protestant, and her children had been christened, but found the local Church of Ireland church did not match their 'outlook'. When they acquired permanent employment in the city, Susan and her husband Graham decided to buy a house, and Graham 'wanted to live in the countryside, not the city'. This white, settled, middle-class family enjoyed a degree of mobility that could support a counter-urban move.[31] This echoes the history of research on rural mobilities and, to some extent, the consumption of a rural idyll associated with green space and quality of life. Susan stated they chose Fairglen school because:

Susan: It's round the corner. There is a nondenominational school in [the city], I think the Educate Together school, but I didn't want to commit the children travelling half an hour each way you know, twice a day. So it's a good school, it's up the road, and you have to weigh the positives and negatives. And because I work part-time, I can walk the children up to school, and I think that's very important, it's a nice start to the day where we can talk.

Susan accommodated the contradictions and constraints of this Catholic school, given the affordances of quality, intimate time with her children and the fact she believed Fairglen was a 'good school'. Put differently, mobilities are afforded in social class terms (property in the countryside, commuting for part-time work). Yet there were traces of immobility in gendered terms, in relation to prioritising domestic over career work – a theme that affected many women. In socio-religious terms, Susan was also acutely conscious of the Catholic habitus of 'the community' and that she would never be 'a local'; but she worked hard for a level of belonging and recognition, that is, to alter what this place means and how it feels:

Susan: On the whole people are very friendly? But some, sometimes, you would realise that you are never, you are never a local . . . I do a lot of work with brownies . . . I know the leader very well . . . and her

	husband was very sick . . . it was only two months after he died, that I had heard.
Yafa:	Wow, wow.
Susan:	. . . I think [if] you're Catholic, you obviously go to mass and that's where you hear, you meet people. It's very social as well as obviously religious . . . I think when you are not in that loop, you are definitely an outsider. But it, it's not too bad like. You can try and try and try, like I'm very involved in the school, I'm on the Parents Association, and . . . I train girls for camogie.[32] Em, because the GAA's huge here. So you can become, you get to be a recognised face.

Getting to know other parents through the school was key for many mothers, regardless of social status or location, to offset relative immobility in the domestic sphere or isolation from the life of the school. Maria was born, reared and worked in the nearby city. She met John, who was from Fairglen, there and moved to Fairglen when they married. Helen was 'from the next parish, I didn't venture very far', but she also attended a city secondary school. Both Helen and her friend Maria, who are Catholic and white-settled Irish, were more comfortable than Susan as locals, and articulated their reasons for sending their children to Fairglen as:

Helen:	Well, It's just convenient really. We live literally five minutes away from school.
Maria:	. . . I just work part-time for my husband [now] . . . but when I was working full-time and your children are minded in the area, so convenience for your child-minder as well.

Both also had children in primary and secondary school. Rather than being actively concerned with the primary school's Catholic ethos, they were focused on securing a positive childhood experience and thinking about secondary transitions:

Maria: Our primary schools are so small that if you're moving up to (secondary) school outside Fairglen, you might not necessarily have a classmate going with them to their school [in the city]. So in my case [my daughter] Siobhán had a friend in playschool she was friendly with from around here was going as well, which made it easier.

Scott, Murphy and Gkartzios[33] note that rural mobilities are not limited to counter-urbanisation, they also involve lateral movement from one rural area to another, and/or returning to one's (family) roots. This theme was clear with Maria (above). Monica, who was white, settled, Irish and had moved from a nearby town to live in an even smaller village nearby, felt that, amongst the parish schools, Fairglen was a comparatively bigger school, which would be less claustrophobic and 'would have better facilities'. Monica was also 'thinking forward', as her eldest son would be attending Fairgen's secondary school in the coming autumn, 'so I would be able to drop them'. The formation of rural attachments, and the tricky intimacies surrounding them, were a major theme for these women in the rural setting. But despite the commonalities between them, Susan could 'never' fully do what Helen (in the next main section) described as going 'with the flow' of the school community, which itself remained synonymous with the parish.

Suburban and town localities

Suburban areas outside of a major city examined in the study tended to be more socio-economically and ethnically mixed. Parents in suburban, town and urban contexts rarely used the concept of 'parish' to define their locality. Many families had moved to Ireland for a better life, and many others had moved from other suburban areas around the city so that they could buy a reasonably affordable home. All families faced varying levels of uncertainty regarding the schools available to them, with a number of schools only recently established.

'Who' constituted the school localities making up the large suburban region in the study was highly complex, and both Catholic and Educate Together patrons had challenges in engaging with plurality in various ways. Given that demand exceeded the number of places in schools in these areas, challenges and barriers for families at the time included the prioritisation of Catholic children in Catholic schools, first-come first-served admissions policies, and the fact that migrant families did not have the same histories or networks as others. Finding a place of immediate belonging was a relief for Katharina (who was white Hungarian) in Raven Hill, an Educate Together school designated as serving a disadvantaged population:

Katharina: There are waiting lists and actually we had three choices, the other Educate Together school and the boys' Catholic school and this one and you know that because everybody was so open-minded and so friendly that's why . . . we decided to come here. The first impression was like, we stopped the car in the parking area, the principal came to say hello and greet us, and everything was so nice.

84

Nicole, who was white, Irish Catholic and had moved from a quite disadvantaged city region in childhood, found gatekeeping in other schools, regardless of ethos, a problem:

Nicole: I went to the Catholic school and got a bad vibe the minute I walked in . . . I found the secretary wasn't very helpful. She was asking loads of questions first . . . And I was saying 'I'm not gonna put a deposit down without knowing what my child is gettin' involved in'.

Karl: Did you feel there was an attitude towards you?

Nicole: Yeah, yeah. That 'she was coming probably from Termonfort' . . . When I went back down and met [Raven Hill's principal], I just got a real good vibe of the school, and he let me look around the school, I got real comfor[t] – I didn't get that from the other Educate Together [Deansfort], it was real again, 'you have to pay the deposit'.

The principal of Raven Hill (disadvantaged, ethnically mixed) Educate Together school was highly aware of how advantaged, and actively discriminatory, some parents were over others, in a context of what he termed an 'exploding' population and the rapid development of new schools across the suburban region:

Principal: 'Choice' means that some people get their choice and some people don't. So the people know the system now to have their children's names down and now to, they know how to work the system . . . the people that don't – they come to other schools . . .

I would still have parents come and [say] 'how many Irish children are in the school?' They know they shouldn't ask that question, but they would still ask.

Parents in Deansfort Educate Together, a predominantly middle-class, white, settled Irish suburban school nearby, were acutely conscious of schools' reputations and their associated neighbourhoods. Therese and Grace (below), both white, settled, Irish and practising Catholics, did not send their children to the closest existing Catholic school (St Brendan's), stating:

Therese: I wasn't specifically looking for an Educate Together. It didn't matter to me really, if (my daughter) could have got a place in (a more middle-class, long established Catholic school in the region), we would have gone there . . . because we are Catholic and we do the religion outside of the school here . . .

Karl: And what was it about St Brendan's, was it too far?

Gina: It's not in a very nice area and that attracts a certain demographic.

Kate: Rough enough, like.

Grace: . . . I chose [Deansfort] because I literally live [next door] . . . at that stage [Deansfort] school had a really good name . . . if there had been a Catholic school at the end of the road I probably would have [chosen that] . . . but [Deansfort] had a good reputation.

Therese: There's a different feel about this place . . .

Grace: It's respectful to [the children] and respectful to adults.

Gina: With their literacy, numeracy, I think they get those skills in any school . . . here I think they're very outspoken, they're not afraid to step up.

Above, the basis of Deansfort's reputation was overtly described in terms of the children's 'outspoken' agency – itself aligned with middle-class-advantaging discourses of individualised school choice and the appearance of self-reliance and responsibility. It was not surprising then that children's outspokenness was encoded in terms of a school context that was not 'rough' or significantly challenging to the status quo in social class terms. The requirement of a Catholic baptismal certificate was outlawed as of October 2018, but the more subtle stigmatisation and immobilisation of families and neighbourhoods through school encounters and parent grapevines, as seen in the 'roughness' attributed to St Brendan's and the 'vibe' felt by Nicole, is harder to challenge.

In contrast to Deansfort parents above, as the Raven Hill principal stated, some parents were not as familiar with 'working the system'. Faith, a Catholic Nigerian woman whose children were attending St Brendan's, which was stigmatised above, did not appear to explicitly consider, or be aware of, prevailing local dynamics in terms of school reputation. Faith's children were not baptised Catholics, as her then-husband was Pentecostal.

Faith: It was the closest school to my house at the time my first son went there. So the rest of [my children] might go there as well.
Karl: I'm wondering . . . why would you not choose an Educate Together?

Faith: We weren't asked questions, like when I brought the children . . . they asked for baptism, if we had them baptised [as Catholics], and I said no. And they [asked] if I want to go away, and I said 'no' and I said 'is that a problem?' and they said 'no'.

A number of parents, including Faith (above), who were of migrant or minority ethnic background, active in religious communities/organisations and linked to socio-economically mixed, suburban Catholic schools, were put off by Educate Together schools because of the importance of the school uniform to them as parents. Urban Catholic schools' material culture was important for certain parents' adherence to traditional values regarding childhood. The importance of the uniform for parents could not be reduced to the saving of labour and expense that having a uniform purportedly allows. The uniform was a tangible artefact that helped assess the school's reputation, in a way that, for these parents, was informed by religious cultural capital developed in countries of origin, that was not as valued in this locality. The embodiment of discipline signified by the uniform was clearly attractive to Nita (Indian) and Ola (Nigerian), in St Michael's and shaped their family's mobility practices:

Nita: I have Inis Educate Together just two minutes' walking but I don't like without uniform, just get ready and come to school. Uniform is a discipline.

Ola: I did not want them to go to the Educate Together . . . I have like two behind my house . . . somebody told me about the new school that was opening here and that it's a Catholic school and that they would wear uniform and I said, well I don't mind the journey.

88

The next section demonstrates some of the majoritarian, contested and, at times, racialised ways in which certain Catholic schools' 'bundle' of secular and religious meanings shaped and affected parents and families.

Catholic Majoritarianism in 'Choice' Dynamics

There was a clear distinction between the Catholic *school* and the Catholic *Church* for parents across Catholic schools, whereby education in the former in no way denoted a lasting or necessary relationship with the latter. This complements O'Mahony's thesis that Catholic schools in Ireland are becoming deprivatised, or incorporating the development of notions of citizenship and rights.[34] But there was little concern shown amongst many white, settled, Irish Catholic parents about how their diverse ways of being Catholic (for example, personal practices, participation in key annual events, daily or weekly mass attendance) related to their typically default reliance on Catholic schools to carry on ethno-religious traditions.

Contradictions in parents' views in regard to enabling children's voices, while seeking/protecting (white) middle-class territory, were evident in the data already discussed. Contradictions in such parents' views regarding the clear lack of alternative schools also became evident when discussing the publicly significant issue of religious instruction and culture in Catholic schools. Parents identifying as Catholic had a variety of views on the Church, faith and childhood (explored in chapter five), but most focused on the importance of annual events, rites of passage and a sense of spiritual comfort that tradition gave them. There were alternatively paternalistic and defensive

89

positions articulated when the topics of including minority religious and non-religious worldviews, and of divesting Catholic schools was raised. Helen (quoted earlier in the Fairglen rural setting) stated:

Helen: I always have this opinion that if children from other communities are coming into the school, they should just go with the flow of the school. Another are kids who don't do religion at all in school, which is their parents' decision sort of thing, but I do think the kids really do miss out.

Sharon, a Catholic, working-class, white Irish mother in the large town setting, was ambivalent about more affluent mothers who were more actively involved in Scoil Cholmcille. But she felt a deep, lifelong connection to the locality and to her son's school, which she herself had attended. While welcoming of diversity in principle, Sharon also focused on the challenges for (white, settled, Irish) Catholic families in a town where there was only one alternative in secular/religious terms – a small Church of Ireland school.

Sharon: When we went to school if you saw a coloured person walking down the street it was like [mock-stares] . . . Cillian's (my son's) best friend is a coloured guy that lives behind us, he's Indian. He has another guy that's French, and he has Polish friends . . . I think it's much better now . . . we didn't have different cultures . . . But . . . when we were in primary school, your Christmas play was the Nativity . . . [the school] was going to stop the

> Nativity because of the different cultures? . . . Why
> should we stop our [culture] just because there's so
> much different cultures coming in? I don't agree with
> it, they don't want to take part, they don't have to.

While the racialised, classed and gendered questioning of
Catholic authenticity is a major feature of public discourse
(see chapters three and five), in local practice, Catholic
majoritarianism was accepted by many parents. This
majoritarianism was both accommodated and subtly resisted
by minority religious parents. Below, Neha, who is Indian and
Hindu, recognises how central institutional Catholicism was
to local reputation, belonging and identity in St Michael's.
Discourses of religious discipline, individual child development,
wellbeing, voice and choice below merged with a wider national
majoritarian backdrop of 'belonging':

Neha: The reason my son is here, because I like the
          religion, whatever it is . . . I grew up as a Hindu, and
          there were boundaries you know.

Yafa: I mean you could have found these boundaries in a
          Church of Ireland school for example?

Neha: . . . What I have experienced is, when I walk into
          [my son's] classroom, there are rules on the wall you
          know . . . I like that. I don't know what other schools
          [do] because I have never been to other schools . . . If
          one morning he comes and says mum, I want to go
          to church, I don't mind. Or if he wants, he is doing
          communion and I'd like to do all that.

Karl: Would you go as far as getting him baptised if he
          wanted to?

91

Neha: If he likes it, I don't mind at all. That's what I want to (do) – understand him as a person.

Karl: Is it more to do with a sense of belonging that you were most concerned with then, than necessarily a particular religion?

Neha: Exactly. I don't mind like . . . sense of belonging.

Some Nigerian parents engaged both African Pentecostal churches and Catholic schools as a way of negotiating the racialised local dynamics of religious inclusion and exclusion. Esther, a parent in Scoil Cholmcille town school, felt isolated from white, settled, Irish neighbours, and the Catholic Church community.

Esther: Father Howard came [to our home] . . . because I used to go to St Joseph's church. But I just stop it for some time and I went to my (African Pentecostal) church in [the city]. And I think they were asking my son Stephen which church do you go to? And my son says we didn't go to this church, we went to church in the city. So the teacher told the Father Howard she doesn't think we are . . .

Karl: Catholic.

Esther: . . . And I explained to Father Howard we are Catholic . . . I told him that I loved to come to their church, but they are not friendly . . . they can't even say 'happy Sunday!' to you. So I'm not comfortable. I told the Father . . . the way they just, not all of them, don't get me wrong, some people say hi . . . [but] the way they just look at you.

While capable of, and needing to negotiate a complex reality, certain minority ethnic parents felt compelled to align themselves with the majoritarian school worldview definitive of the school locality. This was despite the racialised surveillance of Catholic authenticity experienced, particularly by Nigerian families, in both suburban and town settings. In Esther's (above) town, however, a number of parents of migrant/minority ethnic background gravitated towards the smaller, town Church of Ireland school. Church of Ireland primary schools have historically been the only alternative to Catholic schools in Ireland, and specifically embrace an array of Christian churches. As such, they have developed long-standing reputations as catering to more diverse populations.

Openness and generosity towards the Other: Engagement with plurality?

The question of engagement with plurality in a given school context is intimately connected to school type and demographic. As noted earlier, each school setting is a 'bundle' of secular and religious meanings, with contestations of that meaning ongoing. Both white, settled, Irish and minority ethnic parents in Catholic schools blurred the lines between technically private religious/denominational practice and the quasi-public space of education. In the suburban Inis Educate Together, however, some migrant/minority ethnic parents who defined themselves as religious had an alternative perspective. While keen that their children learned about other religions, they distinguished more directly between a common school identity and private religious practice. Faiza, who is Pakistani-British and of Muslim faith, stated:

93

Faiza: I didn't want my children to go to Catholic school or a mainstream religious school. I wanted them to go into the school where they learned about all religions . . . The [personal] religious aspect, my husband and myself, as a family we would teach them.

The public/private distinction was somewhat contested within the same parent group, however. Echoing Hemmings' research on Christian bias in technically secular schools, Safiya, who is originally from Pakistan and Muslim, noted that the school has no prayer areas. But Gabina (also from Pakistan and Muslim) felt this was inappropriate:

Safiya: For Muslim girls and boys, I think in fourth or fifth class [aged ten years plus] they must do prayer. But I think inside the school is not possible, no room, no mosque area? And I don't know they have a church here as well or no?

Gabina: But you know, it's Educate Together, so there is no place that should be for anybody, it will be individual stuff . . . if somebody want to pray.

While Fairglen and Scoil Cholmcille were deprivatised by the rhetoric of inclusion and the more tangible, worldly academic and social development of the child, the orientation of white, settled, Irish Catholic parents that we interviewed towards inclusion of diverse religious and non-religious worldviews could be regarded as minimal at best, and a rhetorical commodity at worst. In Fairglen, Monica stated:

94

Monica: About the Catholic ethos in the school – I like the way that they get kids who aren't making their communion, they still get them involved with it. It's not like they are standing out in the corner, like Billy-no-mates. If they want, if the parents want. They get involved.

Geraldine in Scoil Cholmcille also argued that the school was 'not completely nailed down Catholic'. However, she made this statement from the minimalist definition of inclusion:

Geraldine: There's other religions in here as well, which I think is great, and they're all allowed to have their own freedom of expression . . . they're being accommodated. I think it's fine, it's grand.

At the same time, Geraldine recognised the potential for the religious school to be a space in which children could learn to engage with others through religiosity itself:

Geraldine: In life [my children are] gonna meet people who are very religious and who just aren't, so if they've exposed themselves as they go along to what's out there, from home, from me and from the school, then they'll be more prepared and they'll be able to talk to other people.

Like Geraldine, Monica loved the tradition of first communion. She stated she was 'not much into religion . . . I just want them to be good'. When discussing the ambiguities of her low level of formal religious observance, her sense of spirituality and her love of first communion with us, Monica became somewhat emotional, saying she felt 'like a hypocrite' regarding persisting with first communion. However, this engagement with ambiguity was not common in interviews with parents from Catholic backgrounds in Catholic schools.

Conclusion

As this chapter demonstrates, technically secular education policy enactments are not neutral, nor is there a clearly defined, homogenous public to be educated. Catholic schools – in urban, suburban and rural areas – are now largely places where parents are encouraged, in implicitly, if not explicitly, marketised and individualised terms, to secure their children's belonging and development in historically resonant buildings, using tried and tested methods. Tried and tested methods such as first communion preparation are majoritarian and assimilationist in form, creating dilemmas for families identifying with other religions or none. As such, the scales of locality and nationality are clearly blurred in the sometimes implied, and sometimes explicit, continued assumption that Catholics are white, settled, Irish and vice versa. Educate Together as a patron body also faces challenges, however, in its positioning in the market, and the ways that notions of plurality and diversity are contradictorily deployed as commodities by white, settled, middle-class Irish families who are well-networked, active school choosers.[35]

Engagement with plurality – at least in terms of presumptive generosity towards the other – tended to be regarded in parent interviews as a requirement of minorities, in deference to majority Catholic tradition. The 'common' concern for children's academic and social wellbeing and development was frequently discussed, but in ways that did not overtly acknowledge the pressures on families of minority backgrounds to conform. Still, Susan in Fairglen was magnanimous: 'You need an influx of people with different views . . . but you just have to take people on face value, and people are very friendly. Especially up at the school. I regard them as friends.' As the data demonstrates, there is a need to think about engagement with plurality not simply in terms of religious and non-religious difference, but with and through the lens of class, race and gender injustices. The labour that women do to negotiate tradition, dispersed families and a shifting school and societal landscape was largely assumed, rather than explicitly discussed. The work that racially minoritised families do to 'belong' as Neha said, or 'feel among' as Faith called it, tended to be unrecognised, while the formation of school populations and reputations through class and religion-coded parent grapevines was a constant underpinning theme.

The value of schools – both formally secular and religious – as public places where it is possible to destabilise closed, amoral or fundamentalist worldviews is clear. Amin notes, if spaces such as schools 'come segregated at the start, the very possibility of everyday contact with difference is cut out'.[36] While the concept of the school as public space is important to defend, we must not assume that public(s) involved are formed or accessed on the basis of rational choice and consensus alone. In order for deep engagement with plurality to occur, the policy fantasy of a self-interested Irish citizenry equally competing or voting for their preferred school needs to be challenged in a more sustained manner. Conceptualisation of and engagement with contested, unchosen school publics in policy discourse and policy enactment is crucial. Cohen's argument about the unevenness of *policy* mobility is also worth noting.[37] In the suburban and urban context of pressure on school enrolments, recent legislative interventions on waiting lists and the prioritisation of baptised children may affect overtly physical patterns of mobility, but the stigmatising that occurs when minoritised families encounter certain schools is more difficult to deal with. Additionally, it appears that little intervention has been made in rural settings to support Forum on Patronage and Pluralism recommendations about the deprivatisation of 'Stand Alone' (Catholic) schools.

The next chapter examines how children negotiate institutionalised worldviews and injustices in this postsecular context. As discussed in chapter one, modern societies have historically focused on childhood innocence as part of their desire to reproduce themselves. The book's critical postsecular perspective engages the child as plural, beyond the modern rendering of children as simple, precious and innocent. Children, as plural entities, are continuously entangled in encounters with human others and non-human material (consumer, religious, school) culture. The overarching argument of chapters three and four is that children's encounters with the world, and the ongoing formation of their worldviews, teach a significant amount about the possibilities and challenges of engagement with plurality and modes of ethical accountability to one another in an unjust school system. Rather than progressing or failing to progress through a linear series of socio-religious developmental stages, children are plural; they may pursue majoritarian desires to reproduce societal norms and injustices, and/or they may grow sideways and find creative ways to mediate and contest them. As discussed in chapter four, the book's critical postsecular

98

perspective on nomadic ethical agency centralises encounters and world-making over individual conforming to predefined, absolute moral codes or logics regarding the good and the bad and what affinities one should hold/be capable of. Both chapters have critical implications for the becoming public of school systems. From a critical postsecular perspective, there is an urgent need for policy and political discourse on education to regard children's nuanced experiences of secular-religious relations as public concerns, with the aim of challenging a variety of childhood inequalities, partly forged through the unjust marketisation and privatisation of schooling.

3

Children, Worldviews and Plurality: Growing Sideways

Introduction

This chapter explores how seven- and eight-year-old children negotiate the comforts, paradoxes and injustices of being part of, or excluded from, religious and non-religious cultures through school and beyond. In tandem with chapter four, it examines empirical data generated with children regarding their encounters with a variety of people, places, objects and practices. These include schools, churches, family, friends and the complex dynamics of faith, tradition and consumption found in video gaming, lighting candles, dressing, singing and praying. Encounters with the research team – which altered participating children's school rhythms, and their occupation of school spaces – were clearly a central mediating element of the data generation. Thus, from the outset, it is important to underline a point that is perhaps obvious: adult researchers can never access children's experiences entirely empathically or directly. Jones argues:

> Otherness is not only healthy for children and for child–adult relationships, it is essential to what children are. It should be central to ideas of childhood too . . . Research into children's lives, and adult knowledge of them more generally, should acknowledge that some things cannot be (fully) known about children's worlds . . . This left space for children is politically and ethically vital.[1]

Children's encounters with the world always remain to some extent out of adult reach and, in research narratives, children should not be romanticised or stereotyped as intrinsically more playful in how they encounter the world or engage with difference. This is particularly because children are shaped as growing only 'up' through prevailing (age-related/generational, racialised, gendered and classed) norms and stages of schooling, and understandably seek recognition by reproducing such norms in their own way. A brief example is below. I asked Ronan and Samuel why they took part in an enrolment ceremony organised by their school, St Gerard's, and performed in the parish church. The enrolment ceremony committed them and their families to a year of first communion preparation in second class/grade. They said:

Samuel: If you do the enrolment ceremony you could pass on the class like third and . . .

Ronan: Up to sixth (class) to get your confirmation.

Nevertheless (and perhaps in some ways, as the above quote shows), children tend to be afforded greater space and time to be unknowing, and may play with their dependencies and social norms. Children's otherness or queerness in this regard is often accommodated, even if their experimentation is disregarded as 'childish', or even sometimes inappropriate for their age.

Davis argues that studying childhood offers the chance to 'recapture capacities, insights, sensations and resources improperly erased by the march of secular modernity'. He notes children's fears and desires can be engaged through an array of 'story, symbol, faith, myth, tradition, and discovery'.[2] This array owes much to that which is considered pre-secular and beyond the observable, including folklore, legends and superstitions, where there may be 'multiple meetings with the dark, the unknown, the monstrous, the metamorphic'.[3] Forms of fantasy, myth and wonder were important to the children and were articulated not just through stories, music, toy figures, dance and sport, but also through video games, TV and film. During our research encounters in both religious and secular school settings, children expressed the importance of faith-based, rational, affective and scientific ways of knowing, through the mapping of places, exchanging of words, gestures, tone, laughter, glances and scrolling through digital pictures. Importantly, they generated multiple, often playful, ways of both opening up and closing down encounters with difference, conflict and the unknown, drawing on discourses of reason, science, religion, rights and the nation, to name a few.

Sideways growth and engagement with plurality

Throughout the rest of this chapter, I consider three main themes related to the children's experience of 'growing up': experiences of transcendence, watching/being watched, and the experience of one's body and desires. The analysis underlines the point that children do grow 'up', but prescribed paths from apparent innocence of worldviews to knowingness, and from dependence to independence, are not as straightforward as they seem. Through the themes analysed below, I show how they may grow sideways, finding creative ways of viewing the world beyond neatly religious/non-religious and real/symbolic representations of schools, objects and secular/religious divisions of space. Importantly, the focus on children's encounters highlight how their worldviews, and worldviews themselves, are in constant formation, transition, or becoming. For example, experiences of the transcendent are not solely religious or doctrinal in nature: they may emerge through interaction with video games. Consumer and media artefact items can become a critical aspect of one's expression of faith and family, despite the classed and gendered ways this expression is judged. The critical point is that, rather than necessarily trying to reproduce familial, school or societal norms, children find various ways of negotiating the differences, conflicts and ambiguities that are present both within and across religious and secular settings. In doing so, new forms of relationship to the world and new ideas may emerge, even if fleetingly. Understanding these seemingly innocuous and trivial, but in reality complex and nuanced negotiations, is critical for a becoming public of school systems that meaningfully engages children and confronts unequal childhoods.

Engaging Transcendence: Place, Prayer, Video Game, Postures, Story and Song

The encounter below indicates how relative ambivalence, knowingness and unknowingness about religious piety reverberated across the fieldwork. The conversation below took place in a Traveller Community Development organisation with two Traveller brothers, Michael and Shane, who were eight and seven years old, respectively. We were mapping out places of significance to them using plasticine and drawings. They mapped the urban halting site where they lived, the school, their Grannies' respective homes, and the church. Michael told one story about his family that reflects the accommodation injustice and at times fatal danger that Travellers in Ireland face. We were interrupted by Shane's wry question (below). Shane asked me, rhetorically, in a teacherly tone, what my reactionary comment 'Oh Jesus' referred to.

Karl:	What's the halting site like?
Michael:	It has a trailer and a house but we're living in a house at the moment cause our trailer went up on fire one time. And we got a new one.
Karl:	Why'd it go up on fire, what happened to it?
Michael:	We got a stove in and it was too close to the timber.
Karl:	[quietly] Oh, Jesus, ok.
Michael:	And em, we all got out, thank God.
Shane:	[rhetorically] What's 'Oh Jesus'? [immediately] *Forgive our sins* . . .
Karl:	[wryly] Yes, exactly.
Shane:	. . . *Save us from the*

Shane & Karl: *Fires of hell.* [Shane giggles]

Karl: Are there many people in the halting site?

Michael: Em, there's about 8 bays. Michael Vaughan lives beside us . . . he's bay 8. And we're bay 7. And my uncle's beside us.

I immediately felt the interaction (where a settled, middle-class researcher requires working-class, Traveller children to perform certain forms of knowledge) shift towards Shane's purposes, as he drew me into reciting part of the Fatima Prayer (the name of which I had to look up later). We played with piety and were opened up to differently experienced,[4] but shared, affective flashes of our childhoods, namely images of salvation and damnation. I then snapped back into adult researcher mode, refocusing on the halting site. This was not a conscious choice – it was more of an effort to stay on track and play my researcher role. But arguably attempting to explore what passed between us may have been futile. This flash of recognition was hard to articulate, entangled as it was in images of near-death, blurred adult–child status and, for my part at least, ambiguity and ambivalence about religious piety.

This encounter and others below ground three ideas further discussed in chapters one, five and six. The first relates to the fact that, that which is difficult to categorise or predict is central to our everyday encounters, because every encounter is a relation which may draw out unknown, hidden or forgotten aspects of ourselves. Bronwyn Davies writes that 'even as one anticipates the space of talking to someone new, something surprising may happen . . . a fleeting moment . . . leaves its trace somehow, and the idea, not previously thinkable, emerges'.[5] The 'not previously thinkable' does not necessarily refer to a breakthrough, universally original thought – it could refer to something as simple as sharing a conversation with others with whom we have had little shared life experience. Second, affectively speaking, the above encounter indicates how generational states and categories, when viewed in relational terms (adult–child), are not as fixed as we assume them to be. Rather, they may be blurred and/or re-produced in our encounters. Shane's intervention and giggling also underlines how we constantly 'search for encounters that make us more powerful, more able to act effectively in the world, more capable of joy'.[6] Third, such moments urge collective ethical accountability to share the specific ways of knowing produced and to examine the space claimed or created by various bodies. They also urged accountability to pursue a research dynamic that was appropriate to the situation, and not uncritically to abstract research principles or plans. For example, I (uneasily) facilitated Shane walking around the room and exploring the hall outside while I continued to talk with his brother Michael.

While many children indicated some sort of personal relationship with the supernatural or spiritual – mostly in the form of God or Allah – this figure had an almost mythical or abstract status for most white, settled, Irish Catholic children which was removed from their daily lives. God here was often positioned as a benign overseer and creator, to be encountered primarily at key life stages (see the discussion of 'babies' in the final section). However, Chris (who is of Methodist Zimbabwean heritage) and Tariq (of Muslim Mauritian heritage), in particular, explicitly embedded their understandings of the transcendent in ongoing encounters with family and wider ethno-religious community.

Chris: Sometimes when you die, sometimes God can say you can go back there, but you won't just go back there like how you were, you go back there into someone's tummy, and then you get out and you live your life again.

Tariq: When you die, my dad told me when I was in Muslim school, you have to answer questions . . . then you go to the day of judgement and you have to stand up and you're not allowed to sit down . . . People who are Muslims and they believe in Prophet Muhammed, they will get the water that will make them not hungry forever and forever . . . then you have to cross this bridge and there's like underneath there's a fire. For bad people . . . who do bad deeds, the bridge will be really small, and for people who are very good, the bridge will be like wide.

[Raven Hill]

The same could be said of Shane and Michael, who referred to their sense of 'us' when talking with a Traveller activist, Deirdre, who facilitated part of our interview:

Deirdre: Is religion important in your house?
Both: Yes.
Deirdre: And Our Lady?
Both: Yes.
Deirdre: And who's it important to?
Shane: All of us. Michael has a statue of Our Lady and I have another one.
Michael: You have Our Lady of Fatima and I have Our Lady with d'you know them, what you call them white birds again . . . doves.

107

Shane: Michael has a statue of Our Lord. It's like an ornament.
Deirdre: Who bought it?
Shane: Dunno, I'd say I was only small when people gave me them.
Deirdre: And tell me, do you go to Mass on Sunday?
Shane: Sometimes, the odd time.
Deirdre: What about your Granny?
Michael: Em, every Sunday . . . she has a room filled with holy stuff. She even has a big, d'you know the boards with a picture on it, of St Bernadette.

Joanna, Niamh and Charlie (below) attended Scoil Cholmcille and were quite giddy during our interview. All three girls were brought up as Catholic. Not for the first time across the fieldwork, these children found the intimacy of talking about prayer, piety and togetherness a little too solemn, and sometimes inane. This reflected the fact that it was not unusual for white, settled Irish and European child participants across the study to express mirth when talking about their grandparents' generation's perceived solemn, 'not-normal' levels of Catholicism (see also Jack and Ronan, p.113). Here, we discuss a photo of what appears to be a family holding hands around a dinner table in prayer – creating stories of what is happening:

Niamh: They're like 'it's a special day for us, please be good food' . . . to God.
Karl: Right, do you do that, Niamh?
Niamh: Normal people don't do that.
Karl: Who's normal people?
Joanna: Us!
Karl: Do normal people talk to God?

Joanna: They just say something.

Karl: What would they say?

Niamh: I love you, God, I love you!

Karl: Right, but it's not normal to hold hands when you're having dinner? Do you ever pray before you have food? [no]

Yafa: Not in school?

Various: Yeah we do . . . but not at home.

Charlie: My Grandda does it though.

Karl: Why?

Niamh: He's old.

Charlie: Yeah he is old actually!

Karl: Do you ever pray on your own when nobody else is looking?

Joanna: Before sleep time . . . Hail Mary, Our Father, but in Polish!

Karl: Can you give us a bit of it?

Joanna: Recites Hail Mary in Polish

Karl: Why do you say the prayer?

Joanna: To pray just.

Karl: When do you pray?

Niamh: When I'm alone in my room I go like this [adopts a mudra position with her hands] and talk to God.

Karl: Why do you put your hands like that?

Niamh: It's calmer . . . sarcasm!

Karl: Do you believe in that really?

Niamh: Well it calms me down.

Karl: Is it a prayer thing, or a calm thing, or both?

Niamh: Both.

Karl: Can you do that in church?

Niamh: No I do this. [clasps hands together tightly]

[Scoil Cholmcille]

Through stories about imagined others and herself, Niamh comes to use an arguably shallow embodiment of eastern (Hindu and Buddhist) spiritualities as a way of enhancing her capacity for calm. It is interesting that Niamh consciously moves in and out of 'proper' Catholicism, through the ways she alters her hand gestures – from open-mudra-sarcasm-calm to rigid-traditional-Catholicism. Such moments of parody of piety and spirituality through words and hand gestures raise multiple ethical questions regarding cultural appropriation/othering and religious authenticity. It is difficult to disentangle these questions from one another, and the ways they can be explored in a classroom/curricular discussion cannot be decided entirely in the abstract.

The data above gives a brief indication of how particularly white, settled Irish Catholic children, in their encounters with one another and the research space, moved between the playful and solemn and articulated different, personalised perspectives on religious doctrine and ritual. But the pleasures and fears of the transcendent (for example, experiences of 'flow', unveiling mysteries and stories) were not limited to the officially religious. As Hayse notes in his analysis of gaming, 'simply put, the request for transcendence is a quest for something more'.[7] In children's descriptions of their 'favourite things', video game consoles were often popular. Simulations of the present world (for example, through football video games, military games) arguably offer the opportunity to experience a 'birds-eye view' of a fantasy world or, at least, inhabit a shared subjectivity with an avatar. Discussions of video games – particularly violent or physical ones – indicated how performance of ideal boyhood at times involved using technology to actively fantasise about, and identify with, active masculinity.

In contrast to these performances of growing up (looking forward to 'being a man') and growing sideways (identifying with 'manly' pleasures), shared traditional religious piety could be viewed as 'too much' for some Catholic children. The excessiveness of Catholic piety is gendered – as ageing bodies were sometimes regarded as less capable, or incapable, of exhibiting stereotypically masculine traits: of being active, tough, achieving and dominant.[8] Below, Jack, who is Catholic and from a white, settled, Irish working-class background, connected with his Dad through video gaming. Jack described the piety of his great-great Nan's generation as 'weird'. While agreeing with Jack, Ronan also felt a connection to the transcendent through Mass attendance.

Jack: I just live with my Mum and my Dad is down in his Mum's and I sometimes go down there and my Nan lives in Foster Road and I live in Russell Court and I like to spend time playing my Xbox and playing the Xbox 360. And whenever I go out to my Nan's I always play the PlayStation 3 cause my Dad has Grand Theft Auto and I like it . . . Sometimes my Mum makes me go up [to the park] for exercise and I go up there with my brother.

Karl: Why, is exercise important?

Jack: Yeah, cause I'm always in the house playing the PlayStation.

Karl: It's hard to stop, isn't it?

Ronan: Yeah like, I don't play the Xbox that much, because I only have one game and I'm stuck on a level cause I can't understand their language!

Karl: Do you know anybody that goes on Sundays to church or to Mass?

Jack: . . . My great-great Nan actually always goes to Mass every day, not just on Sundays, every single day, and she's 72. [laughs]

Ronan: Really?

Karl: And what do you think about that?

Jack: I think she's a really Christian.

Karl: And what's your opinion like, do you think it's a . . .

Jack: I think it's kind of weird.

Ronan: I think she's obsessed with it!

Karl: So does anyone go to Mass in your house?

Jack: Mmm, not much, but I don't really want to go to Mass on Sundays.

Karl: Why's that?

Jack: I don't know, it's kind of boring.

Ronan: I kinda like going to Mass . . . I feel blessed there, I like it there. Like I feel like God's talking to me . . . through the cross.

[St Gerard's]

Ronan and Jack's data indicates that paradoxical feelings were possible for children, but not necessarily in a way that built ethical accountability to others. Put simply, we might like something like piety for ourselves, but call it weird when others (for example, older people) perform piety in their own way.

Song was also a significant way of accessing the transcendent, and/or cultivating the performance of first communion, which could, for some, enhance their capacity for joy or being 'happy'. As noted in chapter one, first communion ceremonies (which are generally musical affairs) have been quasi-public events in Europe since the sixteenth century. Unsurprisingly, sometimes children spontaneously burst into song as we discussed religious preparation.

Niall: [sings] *As I kneel before you, as I bow my head in prayer, take this day, make it yours and fill me with your love. Ave Maria, gratia plena, Dominus tecum, benedicta tu*. I can't really remember the other part of it.

David: It's actually a song for our communion I think . . . but we're just practising it to get it all right without looking at it.

Karl: How does it make you feel?

Niall: Happy.

David: . . . and I have a question [comment] for you.

Karl: Yeah?

David: We don't really know stuff about our communion because we didn't do it yet.

[St Gerard's]

David's frank confrontation of 'not knowing' was understandable given the middle-class, adult-centred requirement of the research space for children to perform their knowledge of religion and worldviews. 'Not knowing' can be a safety net for children who are part of the majority group, and not knowing can be an articulation of openness, excitement and exploration for anyone, regardless of age. But for children of minority backgrounds, 'not knowing' they would become categorised as Other in their (Catholic) school as they grew, and the very fact of ongoing othering itself, was sometimes upsetting, and persistently difficult. Yafa's interaction with Cormac below is quite a compelling example of his growing sideways – imaginatively engaging with myth, monsters, colour, furniture and equipment in a way that critiques the controlling, overly solemn gaze of Catholic majoritarianism and of human adults, and that makes space for children themselves to see what is happening. On the other hand, Muslim children and families participating in our study were more consciously embedded in ethno-religious communities and devout practices than the majority of (mostly white, Irish) Catholic children. The former children often adopted a pedagogical stance towards the research team (especially me), and regularly conveyed Islamic teachings and practices from their own life experience. Being knowledgeable about faith, and reproducing that knowledge, was important to them in our encounters. These issues are explored further below under the key theme of watching and being watched by unseen and/or unknown entities and authorities.

Watching/Being Watched: Finding Comfort and Finding Ways Around Exclusion

Cormac indicated below that he didn't know that he/his family was non-religious until he reached 'seniors' (senior infant class, aged five to six) in Fairglen (rural) Catholic school. Cormac sometimes had to sit passively in the church during first communion preparation. This is illustrative of the injustice of a Catholic- dominated system on the one hand (why should Cormac have to face this realisation?) and the broader paradox of moral education on the other (when does one 'know' one is non-religious?). During one classroom-based session, we asked Cormac's class to individually interpret and add to the design of the building below (figure 3.1) in any way they wished. While we failed, unfortunately, to take a digital image of Cormac's drawing, we have his vibrant account of what he created. Cormac drew a series of alien, vampire and other funny faces looking in the building's windows. While hovering outside the church, they watched everyone inside. Certainly, most children interpreted it as a church and added various features and created various scenes.

Figure 3.1. Building template which we asked children to draw on, colour and interpret.

Yafa: Hi, wow, that's interesting. So what are these?

Cormac: They're faces that me and my friend do all the time.

Yafa: What's that face?

Cormac: That's a vampire face . . . That's a funny face with his tongue sticking out . . . That's an alien . . . That's a normal face where he's like 'awkward'!

Yafa: So why did you draw all these faces in the windows?

Cormac: Cause I just like to create my own stuff . . . there's a face there, there's a face there, there's a face there and there's a face there.

115

Yafa:	. . . What do you think this building is?
Cormac:	A church.
Yafa:	Could it be another thing?
Cormac:	Em, a funny place where you do church and chameleons [comedians] talk . . . chameleons are like people who make you laugh.
Yafa:	. . . Do you go to church?
Cormac:	No.
Yafa:	Do you like going?
Cormac:	Not really, cause I just don't really, well my family doesn't really believe in God.
Yafa:	What about you [do you believe in God]?
Cormac:	Um-um [no]. I didn't know that until I was in seniors . . . I have been to a church a few times like.
Yafa:	Do you like how they [churches] look like?
Cormac:	Yeah they look ok.
Yafa:	Would you change anything in there? Would you paint these on the walls?
Cormac:	Yeah! Cause I just like to have a bit of fun with other people.
Yafa:	And you think that would make the church a little more fun?
Cormac:	Yeah, besides just always always always always being holy.
Yafa:	What's this holy thing anyway?
Cormac:	It's where people have to believe in God but I don't do it.
Yafa:	Do you think is holy a negative thing?
Cormac:	No.
Yafa:	But it's just getting on your nerves?

Cormac: Yeah . . . I would add in a few toys for the baby children, I would add in smaller chairs for people that are really small in the front, so they can see, and I would leave the rest.

Yafa: What about colours?

Cormac: Yeah, I would make it a little bit more brighter . . . I would add red, black, pink, blue, yellow, all sorts.

Yafa: . . . What are these?

Cormac: They're microphones . . . for other people, for the chameleons.

Yafa: What would they talk about?

Cormac: They'd like talk about jokes and other funny stuff.

Yafa: Do you know a joke?

Cormac: I know two. Knock knock.

Yafa: Who's there?

Cormac: Peas.

Yafa: Peas who?

Cormac: Peas let me in, it's freezing out here.

[Fairglen]

After his classmates' communion ceremony, Cormac stated that he always felt like the odd one out. He then expressed an exasperated desire to take part in the sacrament. But as the exchange above indicates, Cormac did not fit in a human-centric agency–structure dichotomy. He did not, and indeed could not, passively accept or reject Catholicism, as Catholicism is not an abstract body of thought. Rather he was experientially enmeshed in Catholicism through repeated encounters with a variety of objects and spaces, despite his nonbelief. Importantly, it is through these objects and spaces that Cormac apprehended and swerved from religiosity and

117

local church rituals. He negotiated the school community's implicit framing of him as a lacking, non-Catholic child through complex imaginary and metaphor. The word 'holy', which we repeatedly heard from some children in Cormac's class, was grating for him (and for Dylan, a Catholic friend who was not a huge fan of the church or school). This word affected Cormac: he repeated the word 'always' in relation to 'holy' and works to imagine the church otherwise. His experimental images of various funny and out-of-place faces offered a sense of potential in the moment that he felt was missing from a place so entangled in his school experience. He drew on references such as 'awkward!' that are heavily popularised in TV and online content. He countered the transcendence of the church with his own fantastic creatures and overturned its formality with jokes. His complex entanglements incited him to imagine alterations to the space and rhythms of the church, and to take care of those yet-to-be-seen others who cannot participate in the church–comedy club. While I wish to avoid making heroes or martyrs out of marginalised children (in a way that oversimplifies their experience), Cormac's work here was arguably an admirable demonstration of ethical accountability towards known and unknown others.

The comforting idea that God 'keeps us safe' and watches over children was a common way that Catholic children described their experience of God, and how they were moved by faith. However, Caoimhe's words in Scoil Cholmcille (below) reflected the ambivalence amongst some Catholic children about the idea of God watching over them. It also reflected the intensely public, adult-centred nature of longstanding rituals like first communion.

Karl: Do ye pray on your own?

Caoimhe: Sometimes, maybe in the morning in my bedroom or at night.

Karl: What would you say?

Caoimhe: I'd say keep me safe through the day and night and try to forgive me for my sins.

Karl: And do you feel that, do you believe all that?

Caoimhe: I don't know whether to or whether or not to believe it, so sometimes I get confused why I'm doing it or if I should be because maybe he mightn't exist.

Karl: Who's he?

Caoimhe: God . . . sometimes I feel like God, Jesus and Mary mightn't exist . . . that's why I sometimes get confused about all that.

Karl: And how do you feel about communion then?

Caoimhe: Umm, well I'll probably just feel alright, doing it. I feel a little bit scared though, because all the people and saying prayers and stuff in front of lots of people I don't know.

Karl: And have you ever told people you feel a bit scared?

Caoimhe: Em, no.

Karl: Why not?

Caoimhe: Because like, then most of the time when I tell people I'm scared they take ages trying to talk me out of it, that's why.

[Scoil Cholmcille]

Children of different ethno-religious backgrounds could come into conflict with each other regarding truth claims, in their pursuit of a desire to reproduce an essentialised worldview/ identity. This conflict was not simply down to abstract religious commitments, but to embodied feeling and racialised and gendered practices of domination in child cultures. Conor, who is white, settled Irish and Catholic, closed down encounters with difference by seeking to explain his classmates' perceived otherness. This drew Majid into a competition with him.

Conor: I know who goes to Arabic school in our class: Kareem and Majid.

Ismail: And me!

Conor: And Tariq.

Karl: How do you know that they go [Conor]?

Conor: [imitating] Because they always tell us 'we're going to Arabic school today, we're going to Arabic school tomorrow . . .'

Conor: But there is such thing as God. That's why there's a book called the Bible. If somebody makes it, that means it's real. There's loads, there's millions . . .

Majid: We have a Qur'an.

Conor   . . . Of stories.

Majid: Yeah, the Qur'an has all the stories from the Bible. All of the other ones. And it has even more.

[Raven Hill]

The concept of sin, and feelings of sinfulness, rarely arose overtly in discussions with children from religious backgrounds. However, all children were acutely conscious of being regarded as 'good' and performing goodness in a variety of ways.[9] The theme of being watched by an unknown or unseen entity or authority extended to CCTV, the Gardaí (police), and judges. Participant children's sense of comfort and safety was not apparent in discussions of CCTV, which arose as they watched and responded to a short film titled The White Dress.[10] In one scene, the central character, an unnamed girl going through her first communion day alone, steals some white ribbons from a pharmacy for her outfit. When we asked children if anyone was watching this character when she stole from the pharmacy, children across different settings referred to CCTV or security cameras. This was despite the fact that there was no visual or verbal reference to such cameras in the film.

Karl:	What was unusual about her communion day?
Diyan:	She was going [by] herself and she was eating things and she stole a ribbon and then she got money and she bought something and she went home.
Karl:	So what's different about her communion day?
Child 1:	Cause she stole something?
Karl:	And why, would you not do that on communion day?
Child 1:	No.
Karl:	Why not?
Child 1:	Because I imagine that would be disrespectful to God.
Karl:	You think so?
Child 2:	Especially on her communion day!
Karl:	And if it was a normal day would it be less disrespectful?
Various children: No.	
Karl:	Who do you think was watching her in the chemist shop while she stole the ribbon?
Lily:	Maybe the boss?
Diarmuid:	Cameras?
Karl:	Did anyone else think there were cameras in the shop?

Various children: Yeah.

Karl: Have you ever been aware of cameras in a shop?

Various children: Yeah.

[Scoil Cholmcille]

The above, which echoed conversations with participant children in other schools, indicates the extent to which the participants were conscious of how (their) conduct is watched in public spaces (and increasingly in intimate spaces, for example, through nanny cams). As the phrase 'especially on her communion day!' indicates, Catholic children were highly conscious that significant element of events like first communion were quasi-public performances of child ethno-religious identity and normality – where they viscerally experienced watching and being watched by their school community and extended families as they took a major step in 'growing up'. In the next section, I focus particularly on Lily, who was the subject of a previous paper regarding the ways in which children may negotiate, be captured by and exceed everyday dynamics of tradition and commodification. This is part of the final theme of this chapter: the ways children negotiated classed, gendered and (a)sexual encounters with bodies and as bodies.[11]

Classed, Gendered and (A)sexual Bodies and Desires: First Communion and Beyond

Moral panics regarding children's engagement with the material culture of religious tradition, and panics over child sexuality, are not simply media clickbait: they are a feature of modernity.

McGrail notes that the trend towards white first communion dresses in eighteenth-century Paris:

> may have been variously interpreted as a counter-sign to the elaborate dress of court society . . . but [the dresses] themselves became fashion items. Meanwhile the white veil was deliberately introduced in the early eighteenth century at St Sulpice (Paris), to counter the tendency to spending several hours immediately before the event dressing the girls' hair . . . The age of reason discourse located first communion at the onset of adolescence [but also] . . . associated the ritual with ecclesial preoccupations concerning the pubescent onset of sexual awareness.[12]

The age of first communion was lowered in 1910 by Pope Pius X, in part due to concerns that the requirement that children reach the 'age of reason' in order receive first communion pushed the timing of the ceremony too close to sexual maturation and away from apparent childhood asexuality. As noted in earlier chapters, contemporary public critiques of first communion ceremonies have tended to focus on the maintenance of the sacrament in a majoritarian school system by articulating often reactionary, classed, racialised, gendered, heteronormative and adult-centred 'concerns' about Catholic family materialism, and inappropriate and unruly bodies. For example, Mary Hanafin was Ireland's Minister of Education and Science (2004–8) and largely fudged the issue of school patronage.[13] In May 2009, Hanafin was supporting a crisis local election campaign, while holding a different ministerial portfolio. She took a break from canvassing to attend a first communion in her constituency. She reportedly felt one of the children was:

Like a little bride . . . The sisters were in psychedelic . . . all I could call them were little bra tops in the church and were in and out and in and out (of the church) – 10 or 11 years of age . . . You can't blame the child for that but you'd love to be in a position to support the parents to know that it's not in their interests.[14]

As I have discussed elsewhere, concern about first communion in Ireland fundamentally articulates concern regarding the ambiguities of contemporary capitalism.[15] The increased availability and array of clothes and new technologies in advanced capitalism means that distinctions between middle-class and lower-income communities have blurred somewhat, as have distinctions between adult and child entertainment and modes of embodiment. Beverley Skeggs and Helen Wood demonstrate that media, including reality TV, is a key ground where audiences are invited to make distinctions between tasteful and distasteful bodies.[16] Among the many things that are interesting about the above report is that the critique of child brides is not a critique of heteronormativity, but rather a critique of heterosexuality being expressed too early, and a failure to perform Catholic reverence at a time of austerity. Post the Celtic Tiger years, politicians and corporate media made more and more capital out of what they presented as tacky and sexualised first communion conduct.

With the above context in mind, the analysis in this section foregrounds the experience of bodies in children's negotiation of religious, spiritual and non-religious worldviews and how they negotiate dynamics of tradition, commodification, recognition and difference. I focus first below particularly on Lily – a white, settled, Irish working-class girl – and her encounters with us and with the sacraments of baptism and communion in some detail. These encounters bring together and extend a range of arguments in this book regarding growing sideways, the significance of memory to being moved/affected in the present (even in childhood), and engagement with a plurality of objects, words and places that both reproduce and challenge classed, racialised, gendered, generationed and heteronormative dynamics of tradition and commodification. Unlike other children identified as Catholic in Scoil Cholmcille school, Lily was the only person in her class to be baptised a few months before her communion. This was unique both in this and in all other Catholic school localities studied, as it did not follow the typical rhythm of infant baptism and first communion seven years later.

Lily: I had to sit down and listen to a story first and then he [Father Green] put oil on us and read us another story . . . Then he gave us oil here first [neck] and oil here [forehead]. And then we went over to the thing [baptismal pool] and he baptised all of us. But when he put water on my head I touched my head to see if it was actually soaking but when I touched it it was very dry.

Karl: . . . And what did he say when he was putting the water on you?

Lily: [performing the sign of the cross] He said 'In the name of the Father, Son and Holy Spirit' . . . and then . . . we all go 'Amen'. But my head was still dry!

Yafa: . . . How did you feel when he did that?

Lily: I feel more better so I could get my communion and my confirmation.

Karl: You felt more better?

Lily: Yeah so I wouldn't have to be worried about my communion and confirmation . . . cause I wanted to make my confirmation with the rest of my cousins and friends.

Yafa: . . . Would it be alright if you didn't do your communion?

Lily: No, I wanted to do my communion anyway.

Karl: Why did you want to do it?

Lily: Cause I wanted to wear my dress and get my hair done and make more money[17] so I could get my phone.

Caoimhe: You're allowed to get a phone, lucky! I'm not even allowed to get my ears pierced yet!

Karl: . . . Couldn't you just get those things like the iPad or new phone or whatever and not make communion like, couldn't you just ask for them?

Lily: Well, my Mam wouldn't be able to get them [any time] cause he [older brother Fergal] has to get food . . . he's gonna get sick if he doesn't eat some things.

[Scoil Cholmcille]

Here, Lily first described her past body's movement towards, paraphrasing Anna Hickey-Moody, a sense of 'wonder at and of worldly surrounds'.[18] She focused on the traditional oil (or chrism) meeting parts of her body, the 'special water', her dry head and prayer rituals. She described a changed capacity for her body: to 'feel more better' through these encounters. Lily's references to these sacraments involves objects and forms of embodiment and social recognition (phone, hair-dos, money) beyond her Catholic school and family context, incorporating peers and global consumer products. These items were variously considered in austerity and authenticity-focused public political culture to be immoral: to signify the commercialisation of childhood and classed in/authenticity of Catholic ritual.[19] But Lily's accounts above and below of death, illness and lack of safety spoke to the nuanced and classed nature of her socio-religious experience. She articulated an anti-individualist desire to care for her community, and a sense of spiritual responsibility that exceeds generational hierarchies. She also demonstrated the affirmative affective force of states of illness and death on her capacity to be Catholic. Lily vividly and uniquely described the purposes to which she put the candle she received towards the beginning of the school year.

Karl: Do you pray at all, Lily?

Lily: Well, remember at church we got candles? . . . and like every night we're supposed to pray and every morning we're meant to pray for people who are, died.

Karl: Do you do that? Yeah. On your own?

Lily: Well my mother would give me a lighter to light it but then she would stay in the kitchen with me.

Karl: What do you say?

Lily: I like pray for people who have died, people of my relation like of Grace Burke, she died and she had three kids but the father heard about it, but he came down all the way from England to collect the kids to bring them up so the kids wouldn't get hurt down here . . . cause their grandda always goes out and he's very silly, he does very silly things when he is drunk. He might hurt the kids so he [the father] said 'I might come down and take the kids'.

[Scoil Cholmcille]

We might not view this description of domestic prayer as evidence that Lily (whose public engagement with Catholic ceremonies was perceived by some as untimely at best) was privately more authentically Catholic than others. The point is that the boundaries between quasi-public bodies and spaces (for example, communion ceremonies) and private bodies and spaces (for example, prayer for the dead in the kitchen) are not experienced as separate; rather they are porous and enmeshed. Furthermore, the focus on the hetero-gendered symbol of the (white) communion dress demonstrates Lily's complex assembling of spirituality, consumption, innocence and knowingness as a kind of growing sideways: negotiating competing messages to look nice and be nice in the right way at the right time. Paraphrasing Emma Renold and Jessica Ringrose, Lily worked at, and sometimes surpassed, the 'repressive constitution of . . . [her]lack in the social' as failing to look nice or be nice.[20] Below, Lily discussed what she wore to her baptism with us. Following this is an image of what she would like to look like on communion day (figure 3.2).

Yafa: So you're going to wear a [white] dress on your communion day then? What were you wearing yesterday [at the baptism ceremony]? Was it a dress as well?

Lily: No a leopard dress.

Yafa: Was that nice?

Lily: [Gestures to her legs] And I wore these leggings cause I've two pairs but I wore the smaller pair yesterday and three-quarter-lengths and I wore high heels.

Karl: . . . I thought you said to me you were going to wear white?

Lily: No I was going to wear white but I didn't want to wear white then . . . I wanted to wear a leopard dress cause I got a new leopard dress, I wanted to wear it.

Karl: And could you wear that for the communion?

Lily: No, cause you have to wear a white dress.

Karl: But you had said to me that you had to wear a white dress [for baptism] Lily. You don't have to, like, only you have to wear white if you're a baby.

Caoimhe: My one's tiny . . . my baptising dress is tiny now, it won't even fit on my leg any more!

                                              [Scoil Cholmcille]

Lily's enfolding in these words, images and materials (her leggings, etc.) exceeded public debates which problematise dichotomies of authentic-practising and inauthentic-non-practising Catholic families, and responsible/modest and irresponsible/excessive displays of girls in public. Lily's encounters with the world were nuanced in ways that collectively queered the temporal order of growing up. They possibly made this order irrelevant, at least in differing moments of experience. Lily did not inhabit an adult state when she talked about death, drunkenness, praying for her community, or wearing a leopard-print dress. Her friend Caoimhe did not inhabit an infant state when she talked about her baptism gown. But they experienced

Figure 3.2. Lily's drawing of what she will look like on first communion day.

being moved, and growing sideways, triggered by the force of particular words, materials and images. Lily was unapologetic about her bodily presentation ahead of communion. Her words did not imply that religiosity, tradition or feeling are backward.[21] Rather, they were unique expressions produced through both generative and restrictive (generationed, hetero-gendered, classed) entanglements with a range of bodies, objects and contexts associated with first communion.

Bodies: real and symbolic, sexual and asexual

Sexuality and reproduction were themes that came up indirectly, but not infrequently, during the research. The conversation below was recorded as Mairead and Alan (both white, settled, Irish, Catholic) set about performing a teacher-set task: illustrating their favourite Bible story. They chose the Annunciation, a story about how the Archangel Gabriel informed the Blessed Virgin Mary that she would conceive and give birth to the Son of God. Mairead and Alan were drawing a picture from their Children's Bible (gifted to all communicants by the parish priest). The Annunciation is one site of important feminist debate about the theology of submission.[22] My attempt to explore what was enacted in the Annunciation was turned around on me – and my own question was reductive. By asking 'do you believe this happened or not', I invited Mairead to analyse the Annunciation literally, as a possibly 'real' event that happened in the chronological past.

Karl: What was the Annunciation about?

Mairead: The Annunciation – read this and you'll find out!

Karl: [reading out loud] *A voice called her name, she looked up, a stranger stood beside her, light shone from his face. 'The Lord is with you Mary', the angel said. 'He is pleased with you, he will make a little baby grow inside you.'* Do you think – wow – God made a baby grow inside Mary?

Mairead: Yes. Do you believe in God?

Karl: I'm not sure.

Mairead: That's a yes or a no [giggles].

Karl: Does it have to be yes or no?

Mairead: Yeah, sort of.

Karl: And do you think that could happen today, that someone could have a baby made by God?

Mairead: Well, every baby is made by God.

Alan: So you could just say everybody's made by God cause we were all babies . . . When Adam was alive, he was like, a man [flips back to Creation story where Adam and Eve are both presented naked in the garden.

Karl: What is?

Mairead: Watch this. It goes further [flipping pages]. See? Disgusting!

Karl: Why is it disgusting?

Alan: They're naked! . . . They should get some more clothes, like.

Mairead: That [pointing to another, clothed, character in the Bible].

Karl: Why should they get clothes?

Alan: Two reasons, because they're naked and they're cold.

[Fairglen]

Here, my secular-rationalist questions were met with other-worldly explanations of creation. The questions of conception and birth themselves sparked other ideas and feelings about bodies and sexuality. The children giggled as Alan flipped through the *Children's Bible*. At the same time as they desired the figures to be clothed, asexual and not 'disgusting', Alan felt the desire to point them out in the first place. Since sexuality was in some ways 'beyond the scope' empirically, I did not explore such questions further. However, on reflection, this and other conversations raised questions of modesty and desire that are, at best, relegated to sexuality education curricula which often fail to engage religious worldviews in a systematic way. They demonstrate the need to think in inter- and intra-disciplinary ways about sexuality and religious and non-religious worldviews.

As discussed in the Introduction, understandings of what bodies are, real and symbolic – and the slippage between the two – can be explored and experienced not simply through language in the research encounters, but through the affective relations these encounters engender. This includes exploring ideas and memories of past experiences. Below, Amelia rejected the idea that the bread and wine were the real body and blood of Christ, something that did not appear to be explored officially at school.[23] This spilled over as it were, into a conversation about worldly pleasures: 'real' champagne.

Yafa: What's the holy bread?
Rosella: A part of God's body?
Amelia: Some people say that but I don't think it is . . . I don't
           think it's a piece of God's body.
Yafa: No?

133

Amelia: Because it's just like bread. Our bodies are just like bones and blood.

Yafa: . . . So what do you think it is?

Amelia: Just bread, with holy water.

Rosella: I don't know why they drink wine then so.

Karl: Are you allowed to drink wine?

Rosella: Drink champagne.

Karl: Champagne?

Rosella: Cause it's kids' champagne.

Karl: Where did you drink that?

Rosella: Em, at the new year's party and on my birthday.

Yafa: How did it taste like?

Rosella: Bubbly.

Yafa: Did you like it? [yes]

Karl: Could you bring kids' champagne into the church?

Rosella: No I don't think so.

Amelia: If you had it in a little cup with a top on it, no one would notice and you just drink it.

[Fairglen]

Such encounters create possibilities of exploring further ways we can think about being ethically accountable to one another and engage with plurality. For example, we could consider in the classroom how kids' champagne and blessed wine might be similar and different, and how and why access to these varies cross-culturally and historically. Indeed, blessed communion wine was a part of early Roman Catholic infant baptism rituals, and continues to be a part of infant communion rituals in Orthodox churches.

Conclusion

Children's encounters with the world and their personal worldviews teach a significant amount about the possibilities and challenges of engagement with plurality and modes of ethical accountability to one another. The above analysis demonstrates that children's encounters with the world, rather than signifying intrinsic differences between generations and socio-religious groups, are entirely made in relation to one another, and suggest the possibility of exploring lateral points of connection between generations and socio-religious groups, to challenge assumed knowledge which underpins hierarchies of generation, gender, race, class and religion in schools. Children and adults have ongoing encounters with persons, objects, images, ideas and places that are to lesser or greater extents conscious and intentional, and that may be cast as not of their generation, or something they are not capable of.

Our research encounters brought up unexpected themes, imaginaries and desires, which involved negotiation of tradition, consumption, inclusion and exclusion, such as imagining a church/comedy club, enjoying a leopard-print baptismal dress, playing with religious verse, being watched by CCTV on first communion day, drinking kids' champagne at church and massaging God (chapter four). The children constantly moved within, across and outside the boundaries of organised worldviews and engaged with the known, new and unknown. Through this chapter and the next, I contend that deep engagement with plurality must not simply acknowledge that children make meaning from and participate in the world: it must engage sideways growth and multiple, shifting potentials of our relationships and ethical accountabilities, in order to understand the paradoxes, challenge the injustices, and complicate dichotomies of secular/religious school culture in Ireland and elsewhere.

4

What Matters? The Plural Child and Unequal Childhoods

Introduction

This chapter examines more closely children's ethics from a critical postsecular perspective. It contends that values and ideas regarding religion, reason, science and rights, coalesce in ways that we cannot always predict in advance. Following on from chapter three, I examine how children's encounters may open up ethical relations with multiple values, ideas, bodies, places, locations and forms of belonging, offering creative, relational ways of being in the world. I also examine how these encounters may close down ethical relations with ideas, bodies, places and values. Notably, the question of ethics and 'what matters' is a question of citizenship, in the sense that it refers to our obligations to known and unknown others, and to the cultivation of rights, belongings, affinities and commonalities. As noted in chapter one, citizenship is not reducible to legal status. It is socio-cultural, affective and multi-layered (for example, religious, economic, generational). Forms of access and claim to, and experiences of citizenship, are shaped by many socially created hierarchies, including those of class, race and gender.

The chapter explores how children's capacity to engage with a variety of ethical issues or 'things that matter' is enabled and constrained, thus demonstrating the forms of relationships, belongings and accountabilities available to, claimed and enacted by them. While the question of 'what matters' includes an almost limitless array of issues, the themes explored in this chapter were (1) belonging, class, consumption and poverty, (2) moral judgement and (3) living a good life. Analysis of these themes shows, as with chapter three, that child cultures are sites of struggle where those taking a majority or majoritarian position can more easily resist explicitly engaging plurality, or finding affinity and commonality.

While the data below is not intended to be generalisable to all experiences of childhood in Ireland (and such generalisations are often unhelpful), the majoritarianism evident in this chapter and across previous chapters does support the argument that a state level Education about Religion and Beliefs (ERB) and Ethics curriculum is long overdue. But as with the Introduction and chapter six, I argue that meaningful engagement of children's ethics, agency and citizenship, in public education, rather than being *entirely* modelled on an individualist notion of the child at the centre of a fixed set of moral concerns, must be rooted in multiple and mobile interrelating encounters and affiliations, where experiences of place, identity and belonging are felt, defined, imagined and contested on an ongoing basis. Before analysis of the data, it is important to outline this critical postsecular view of children's ethical agency and place in the world, to distinguish it from prevailing, binary conceptions of the child being on the periphery/at the centre of fixed notions of morality and commonality.

Ethical childhoods and commonalities: Placing children at the centre?

Formal moral education, as it developed in nineteenth- and twentieth-century Ireland, was confined largely to faith formation. The majority view of a 'good' Irish childhood was one which involved initiation into full membership of the Catholic Church, through baptism, and then via schools, through first communion and confirmation. Irish parochialism and moral communitarianism reflected not just strictly religious goals, but selective modernising economic, social and cultural adaptations in Ireland under both British and Irish states. These adaptations confined 'proper' childhoods away from public, adult life, focusing particularly on schools.[1] While children and childhood were in theory cherished in this process, they were not at its centre. In contrast to a secular–liberal individual view of the person, and in common with many religious traditions, children's faith formation ideally existed with and for the ethno-religious community and transcendent goals. But the abuse, poverty and fear perpetrated against many children, women and vulnerable adults through schools and parish structures in Ireland reminds us how collectively violent and dehumanising educational subsidiarity and moral communitarianism can become.

Since the 1970s, we have seen a slow process of centring of child development and, more recently, children's rights and citizenship in national school curricula and education policy. This centring of children and childhood has been typically based on

139

secular (psychological, developmental and rights-based) views of the individual unitary self as situated at the core of broader, worldly, interconnecting scales of moral commonality: family, school, community, nation, humanity. The focus on citizenship and rights has in particular been apparent in recent years in the Forum on Patronage and Pluralism report and the development of a framework for Ireland's first ever Education about Religions and Beliefs (ERB) and Ethics curriculum. There is much to be celebrated in the secular framing of the child as a full individual with rights and affinities with others as local, national and global citizen. But as noted in the Introduction, this framing is not culturally neutral, and tends to depend on a conception of agency and freedom that downplays deep attachments and affinities, particularly those relating to the religious and transcendent.[2] Additionally, neoliberalism's framing of child development as something to invest in, and to maximise emotional and financial value from, implicitly underpins contemporary policy emphases on child citizenship.[3]

While traditional religious views tended to place the child at the periphery of moral concern and communitarianism, secular modern paradigms place the child at the centre of a range of local, national and global circles as a moral project in and of itself. But as discussed in the Introduction, the secularist narrowing of the 'I' to the individual child who is central to, but ultimately becoming individualised from, their external world can narrow what is possible for a child to become. It can downplay pre-verbal/pre-personal (religious) attachments seen in the Introduction and chapter three, fall prey to neoliberal values of self-interest, freedom and productive development, and fail to engage with the lived ethics of childhoods and imaginative, collective, human and non-human forms of ethical agency which place encounters, and not an rigidly individual concept of the human, at their centre.

This book's critical postsecular perspective takes a lead from Gilles Deleuze's and Rosi Braidotti's respective work on *nomadic* ethical agency as being distinguishable from prevailing secular-Christian individual moral agency.[4] 'What matters' in nomadic ethics is not focused primarily on moral rules, assumptions or commonalities that predefine good or bad individuals in fixed, universal ways. Rather, what matters *is* matter: world-making, and the cultivation and experience of plural encounters through human and non-human material culture. This is not a relativist stance that ignores commitment to religious, spiritual and non-religious worldviews, communities and values. Braidotti argues rather that ethical behaviour in this view 'confirms, facilitates and enhances the subject's *potential*, as the capacity to express his or her freedom',[5] through their encounters with human and non-human, known and unknown others. An example of the capacity to express one's freedom is below, where Mairead demonstrates, verbally and non-verbally, how being fun and being holy are entirely compatible.

Karl: Is the church a fun place? [Chorus: Nooo]
Children: No!
One child: Yes!
Karl: What do you mean when you say it's not a fun place?
Cormac: Em there's nothing fun about it, it's just always holy.
Karl: Ok, so right. Can you be holy and have fun at the same time?
Others: Yeah.

Karl: Ok so you can do that, how could you have fun and still be holy?

Mairead: You could sing being holy like 'praise God'. [humming, raising her arms and moving her body in the seat]

Karl: Can you dance and be holy?

Children: Yes [some laugh].

[Fairglen]

Braidotti argues that acknowledgement of our entanglements with human and non-human, known and unknown, others can increase 'the range and span of interconnections and hence of ethical agency'.[6] Being facilitated to be fun and holy – to move when praying – would increase the range and span of Mairead's relations to clergy, the Church and vice versa, and thus potentially create a new or broader range of relationships. Finding out what matters and engaging with plurality, then, is not about being entirely beholden to abstract moral (secular or religious) principles, and a circumscribed set of communities – it is about an ongoing process of exploring/encountering ourselves and other bodies, ideas, objects and places. Of course, those encounters involve negotiation of classed, gendered, racialised norms regarding who belongs where, and may repeat these norms and/or try to depart from them. As another example outlined below indicates, the process of deciding 'what goes in the middle' of our map is a collective process of encounter and negotiation where new ideas and imaginaries of relationships can emerge or be closed off.

What Matters? Messy Secular and Religious Geographies of Belonging

Public and political debate on religious education tends to focus on the content of faith formation versus education about religions and ethics, with little empirical analysis of the lived, messy experience of either. Below, we asked Grace, who attended Catholic class after school in Raven Hill Educate Together, to explain her experience of learning *about* religion in school and learning *in/through* religion after school. During the particular encounter below, Grace identified more with her Catholic afterschool class – and notably this conversation occurred the day after her first communion with a small number of Catholic Educate Together classmates. Grace articulated a desire for cultural Catholic reproduction (learning 'the same thing'), and she favoured her apparently 'small-voiced' afterschool Catholic teacher. Grace also favoured the idea of learning from co-religionist adults 'about God' in Catholic class, rather than *about* religions from non-co-religionists under the Learn Together curriculum. She moved around the room to articulate her view, using toys as props, taking on the role of her different teachers and role-playing 'what Catholics do' from an emic, or insider, perspective. This included singing (religiously), and even cleaning:

Grace: In afterschool we know what we're doing already . . . every Wednesday, we have to learn the same thing for the communion.
Karl: Which class do you prefer, your school class or your afterschool class?

143

Grace: [preparing to get into role] Afterschool class now. I'm
            your teacher (high-pitched voice). 'Ok, class, today
            we are going to be learning about . . . [deliberate
            pause for effect] God!'
Karl: Do you like the way she teaches?
Grace: Yeah, she asks in a small voice . . . she keeps
            like, she has God on the board already, and then
            we read it, and then my (school) teacher goes in a
            loud voice . . . 'I'm your teacher and we're going
            to be learning about . . . France!' . . . Will I tell you
            why it's kinda weird that we learn about religion in
            school? Cause like we're not, we're supposed to
            learn about school stuff but that's also school stuff,
            but the parents don't know that they're teaching us
            (about religions) . . . If we were doing (learning as)
            Catholics, Catholics sing a lot! Now I am doing, like
            Catholic people also like cleaning!
Karl: So what's different in the after school?
Grace: Cause they like, they act normal. They make a slow
            voice – what would you do if your teacher said –
            you're in school and you don't know anything about
            Catholics ok?

                                                        [Raven Hill]

Grace's mention of 'God on the [white]board already' appears
to refer quite literally to a chalk and talk approach, which is not
recommended in Ireland's Catholic preschool and primary-
school education curriculum.[7] Her desire to be part of a Catholic
learning community first and foremost – articulated through role
play – was both a legitimate articulation of common identity and
another reminder of the dominance of the majority culture in the
local area. At the same time, in the Catholic afterschool class

144

that we observed, Grace directly challenged the teacher and priest on their explanations of the afterlife. In a research-based activity where we examined the life course (discussed in the last section of this chapter), she also felt that when people die, they die – with no afterlife. Grace thus was plural herself.

The first research activity we conducted with each class group was a local mapping exercise, which began an exploration of secular and religious forms of belonging in everyday life. Tying in with chapter three, the mapping exercise had a significant role to play in sparking discussions regarding who or what, if anything/anyone, 'watches over' the participating children, particularly in Cormac's school (Fairglen, rural Catholic). We asked children to look at and discuss photographs of the local built and natural environment (for example, the school, residential areas, shops, parks, fields, swimming pools, religious buildings). This supported the children in making the local environment concrete, and creating their own map with plasticine, straws, crepe paper and drawings on a giant sheet of paper. Each group discussed and voted on what they would put at the centre of the map.

Karl: Would anyone else think we should put the church in the middle?

Brendan: [hand up] Oh, oh!

Karl: Brendan?

Brendan: Because em, [God's] in the middle and he's like keep us safe [sic] all around us.

Child 1: Cause it's in the middle of Fairglen . . . the church.

Karl: OK. And what other ideas do we have?

Max: Em . . . Spar [local shop].

Child 2: That's cause his dad works there!

[Fairglen]

145

Both materially and symbolically, the Catholic church was at the centre of how community was defined not just amongst adults in Fairglen, but amongst Catholic children in this rural setting. This was unsurprising, given the significance of the parish structure in defining boundaries in people's everyday language in this rural context (as noted in chapter two). One could argue that the settings represented on the map indicated that the values that children live by are entangled with their most intimate experiences (of family/home, health, and religious community). However, the children were not trapped by these entanglements. Extensions of that conversation sometimes helped think of other affinities, and ways of living through different sites and geographical scales, even if these affinities did not have a social justice orientation. One could argue that, below, the children imagine other 'little public spheres', as Anna Hickey-Moody describes it – living together around the cinema (which is at least twenty minutes' drive away), for example.[8] These extensions of the conversation were important to exploring different ways of thinking about living and belonging together, and finding pleasure and joy.

Yafa: Why would you put the cinema in the middle?
Aoibheann: If we could put all the houses outside, everyone could drive into the middle.
Karl: Aw, you mean where you live, is it?
Aoibheann: Yeah.

[Fairglen]

A somewhat grown-up rural fantasy is emitted here – being able to position our houses collectively so that we would be equidistant from the cinema. Of course, part of the challenge in imagining and finding further spaces of common interest (to the school) is the fact that they are often already consumer/commercialised sites, where children's activities are also closely monitored.

During the process of map-making in Raven Hill Educate Together school (below), the participating children drew their own homes or made them out of plasticine and straws, despite being 'prompted' to examine a range of photos of the local area (supermarkets, parks, etc.) on tablets beforehand. The process of encounter here, at least on the surface/at the beginning, tended towards producing an individualised, but careful and dedicated focus on 'my home' and 'my life'. But the process also facilitated something more – it invited encounters with criss-crossing forms of child participation and belonging on ethno-religious, sport/leisure and consumer grounds.

Karl: You've made some beautiful progress . . . Most people made houses, right? How come you made houses and not anything else that was shown on the [tablet]?

Faith: Cause when you're trying to make a house it's kind of hard and you don't really have time.

Karl: What else would you like to make if you had time?

Child: I'd like to make a swimming pool.

Karl: Where do you go swimming?

Child: We go swimming in [south suburb].

Karl: Faith, you said a church?

Faith: Cause you learn about God and stuff that God used to do when we didn't exist.

Karl: What kind of things?

Faith: Like when Moses died.

Karl: . . . Do any of the rest of you know any places where people pray?

Tariq: A mosque.

Karl: Is there a mosque here? Do you want to put down a cup to show us where it is? [yes] And what would you draw on the cup to show it's a mosque?

Tariq: Em, a Muslim symbol?

Karl: Do you want to put a Muslim symbol on it? [yes] Any other place that people like to go to that isn't on the map?

Conor: The church beside my house and supermarket to get my hair cut.

Karl: Is that St Matthew's Church?

Conor: Yeah.

Karl: And do you go there?

Conor: I went there yesterday.

Karl: To Mass? And did you like that? [yes]

[Raven Hill]

Such invitations to extended conversation could productively blur the lines between secular, religious, public and private experience. There were many religious spaces, including Methodist churches and mosques, in the region which do not have the same visibility as the Catholic churches. When Tariq (above) was invited to add the mosque to the map, he took a white plastic cup, turned it upside down and printed Arabic figures on the side, and wrote 'Mosque' on top with a marker (see figure 4.1). This was significant, given that, despite the diversity of the population, there was no publicly visible mosque in the local area. The act of placing oneself by placing the mosque-cup draws out ethno-religious difference and makes it

148

Figure 4.1. Tariq's representation of the mosque in the local area

a more visible part of this diverse locality – which Conor quickly added to in terms of the Catholic church and supermarket. This blurring of the boundaries of public and private space is continuously necessary, when we consider that Ireland's imagining of a secular, public 'we' is mediated through the lens of a white, settled, Catholic notion of a common history.

As previously discussed, children's encounters with the transcendent were playful, spiritual, superstitious and unexpected, reimagining familiar religious spaces and the boundaries of what is sacred from a multi-generational and plural perspective. The extract below emerged from a discussion about the kinds of spaces children do and do not have access to, and what spaces and places they share affinities with. Chloe, Mairead and Alan in Fairglen regarded churches as open to them, but the inaccessibility and solemnity of church spaces was a recurring issue (alluded to in Cormac's experience in chapter three).[9] Echoing broader white, settled, Irish Catholic trends privileging individual spirituality over formal religious observance, access to God for these children was easy – bypassing phallocentric symbols of religious identity (the tall church, etc.).

Karl: Why did they build (churches) so tall?
Chloe: Because they wanted to reach up to God! [playfully reaching up to God]
Karl: . . . If you were to go higher and higher would you meet God?
All: No.
Chloe: Because God is always around us [pretends to massage God's shoulders].
Karl: . . . Are you doing a massage on him? Could you ever actually meet God?
Chloe: He is always around us.
Mairead: . . . He is in the walls, the air.
Karl: If you wanted to talk to him, do you need to do anything special, is he just going to hear you?
Mairead: You pray to him and he hears you.
Karl: Do you have to do a prayer or can you talk like we are? Do you have to hold your hands together?
Mairead: You don't have to do that.
Alan: Sometimes.

[Fairglen]

As noted in chapter three, the church was viewed as central to the map of Fairglen, but clearly, in a globalised world, children's encounters are not simply with proximal people and objects and buildings created using locally sourced materials. Ansell argues that children:

> encounter near and distant places in multiple conscious and unconscious ways. While their most intense interactions may be with proximate spaces, the world they encounter is produced through diverse interactions and they constantly engage with things that connect with distant places – books, school curricula, fruit or clothes produced elsewhere.[10]

Even within the most intimate space of the home, children are entangled with a range of ideas, objects and places, screens and platforms that flow through the globe. In Scoil Cholmcille, the local town clock tower was a catalyst to imagine and place a range of towering world figures and monuments on the map. Through the affective force of the tower, and the image of the Eiffel Tower, children here simultaneously plugged into secular western cultural icons and imaginaries of progress and individual liberty. These imaginaries, while not necessarily central to their everyday sense of belonging and identity, became a significant element of the map they made. Indeed, the Statue of Liberty was voted by most to be placed in the centre of the map, and a few children (boys in particular) led the flight into building western, phallocentric, icons.

Joanna: The big clock in the middle of the [town].
Various children: The clock tower.
Child 1:   The school?

Yafa: So we have clock and school?
Child 1:   The Eiffel Tower?
Yafa: Any other suggestions?
Ciarán: The Eye of London? The London Eye.
Joanna: The Statue of Liberty?
Yafa: Where is that?
Joanna: It's in New York.
Yafa: And is New York in Ireland? [no] Where is it?
Robert: America.
Yafa: And is America far away from Ireland?
Various children: Yeah. Not really.

[Scoil Cholmcille]

Another activity conducted with children involved watching and responding to the animated video 'The Memory Box', part of a series of videos called 'Abbi's Circle'. The video series, produced by Pivotal Arts, explored issues of family migration and injustice. It focused on Abbi, a black-Irish girl of Nigerian descent living with her mother, while her father lived in Nigeria. In 'The Memory Box', Abbi hopes that her father can get an Irish visa to attend her graduation. When his visa is denied, Abbi puts some of her most precious memories and experiences of Ireland into a box for her father. Questions of national belonging and the articulation of multiple ways of being Irish and African tended to follow from this video across rural, urban and suburban settings with different results. Below, in the entirely white, settled, Irish/European Fairglen classroom, the conversation focused almost entirely on testing aesthetic (visual, auditory) markers of sameness and otherness. Below, Sinead's intervention provides the opportunity to open up ethical relations around prevailing assumptions that Irishness involves sounding a certain way (for example, like a character from a 'Sminky Shorts' video).

Yafa:	You said they don't sound Irish. What do you mean by that?
Alan:	Well some people sound Irish and some people sound as if they're from different countries.
Yafa:	Can you give me a sentence where you would sound Irish?
Alan:	I can't do it.
David:	[Referencing 'Sminky Shorts'] *Howarethebois?*
Sinead:	I have a friend and she's living in Ireland and her mum I think is from India . . . she was born in India and she's living in Ireland now.
Karl:	. . . So do you think she's Irish maybe?
Sinead:	I don't know.
Karl:	If you live in a country long enough, even if you're born somewhere else, can you become Irish?
Various:	Yeah.
Child:	You can be born in India and become creshened [christened] in Ireland.
Karl:	Yeah. And can you become Irish then?
Child:	You are Irish . . . if you're creshened somewhere and you speak that language.

[Fairglen]

Alan's admission 'I can't do it', that is produce an Irish-sounding sentence, speaks to the futility of generating one, stable auditory (and, arguably, visual) marker of national character. However, the notion of needing to be christened and speak the native language articulated above closed down possibilities for troubling national identity once more. In Raven Hill Educate Together, Faith and Chris, who were cousins of Zimbabwean descent, were visibly affected by what appeared to be a relatively rare representation of an African Irish child and family through the 'Memory Box' video. Encounters with the same video in this different, suburban school context opened up further possibilities for empathy and ethical understanding:

Karl: Why would [immigration control] stop you from coming?

Chris: Cause maybe the mayor didn't want you to come to the country cause you're not like one of them.

Faith: I think it's kind of harsh . . . Cause if someone really wants someone to come to their graduation, and they can't come cause the person denied it . . . they won't be able to see them.

Karl: Do you think it should be different?

Chris: Yes I really think it should be different cause someone could cry like 'My dad's gone to Morocco, I want my daddy back!' and you won't get him back.

[Raven Hill]

What Matters? Consumption, Class and Poverty

First communion was a theme that provided a vehicle through which children articulated different views on money and spending. Some regarded respect for money as a moral issue in a somewhat privileged way – where there was a common assumption of financial indiscipline amongst those who were less well-off and who appeared to waste their money. For example, after watching the 'White Dress' video, Orlaith stated:

Orlaith: When she came out [of the church] a man gave her some money and she just wasted it on chips [fries]. If I was her I wouldn't spend it on chips.

Karl: I see. Why is it a waste to spend it on chips though?

Orlaith: Because like it's just chips and like she stole the ribbons she needed and she didn't really need the chips . . . because she has loads of things at home.

[Fairglen]

The video was quite clear that this girl did not have 'loads of things at home', but, even if she did, it was notable that the assumption that 'having things' meant one was financially and personally secure was common across different settings. As the discussion of Lily's experience in chapter three indicated, an interesting set of dynamics opened up regarding the clothes that Catholic children would wear on first communion day. A third video that we examined with children across participating schools was a short advertisement from 2009 by the global homeware company Ikea, which targeted people living in Ireland. This commercial promoted the opening of Ikea's first Irish store in greater Dublin that year. Set to the tune of the 1968 song 'Make Your Own Kind of Music', the commercial opens on an idyllic rural church scene, complete with an old Telecom Éireann[11] phonebox nearby – a code for a more innocent, twentieth-century Ireland. In the ad, parents and grandparents talk excitedly while waiting for the priest to lead a group of young white girls wearing traditional first communion dresses and veils in pairs down a lane to the church. The girls wave and adults wave back, proudly taking videos and photos. Then, some people's faces fall, as they notice a red-haired girl without a veil, wearing a red, white and navy polka-dot dress, standing out from the others. The red-haired girl and her (apparent) parents smile happily while other children and adults are taken aback. As the track hits the chorus 'Make your Own Kind of Music', the slogan 'Bring Out Your Rebel' appears. It closes with a Scandinavian-accented voiceover on a modern, furnished living space, advising viewers to 'furnish your home to fit you, not to fit in'.

The video provided a great opportunity to explore the national(ist) symbolism of first communion in Ireland, in large part because it was not targeted at children.[12] Prior to watching the video each time, we displayed a still image from the ad of the aforementioned girl, on her own, waving, without the context of the wider video. This image allowed the possibility of imagining her in terms of her name, age, favourite people and interests. Reflecting the importance of their family relationships, the children imagined her as being at the park, swimming, and that her favourite people were her Mum, Dad, Granny and Granddad. In Fairglen, the footballers Suarez and Gerard were added to her list of favourite people. When we then played the ad and children saw her walking with the group of girls wearing traditional white dresses, no one initially imagined that she was anything other than Catholic. Reasons suggested for why she was not wearing a traditional dress while holding hands with the others included that she was going to make, or had made, her first communion (as an older or younger friend or sibling to the other girls), or that she was a flower girl at a wedding. In Fairglen, one child did suggest she had 'not been christened', while others suggested she could not afford a first communion dress. In fact, a number of children were very conscious of the question of affordability and economy in relation to first communion.

Aoibheann: I think she *was* making her communion, but her communion dress was too much money.

Karl: Does that happen sometimes?

Two/three children: Yeah.

Karl: And what do you do in that case?

Aoibheann: Just try and find a white dress.

Karl: Why would they be too much money? Are they expensive?

Two/three children: Yeah.

Mairead: They're two hundred euro.

Aoibheann: Sometimes when I go to the shop I see communion dresses.

Karl: Oh right and you see the prices on them? [yes] And what do your moms and dads say about the prices? Do they ever talk about the prices on it?

Child: I do.

Child: My sister she made her communion last year and you know the dress, she passes that on to me and I pass it on to my other sister, she passes it on to her other sister.

Yafa: Oh right, and why did you do this?

Child: Em, so we don't have to waste all our money on buying.

[Fairglen]

One can understand the above reluctance to challenge the orthodoxy of the white dress as a ritual symbol of 'doing childhood' or 'doing communion' correctly for a few reasons. A number of girls received their first communion dresses as hand-me-downs from mothers, siblings and cousins. Others received a new communion dress that, to varying extents, expressed their belonging to their family and first communion cohort, while referencing their own tastes. But when asked to draw what they thought they would look like on first communion day, a significant number of children showed the capacity to express themselves differently, depicting a variety of colours, clothes and accessories. Many of these expressions challenged tropes of innocence and solemnity that first communion clothing has historically sought to project.

Max: I just did random colours.
Karl: Are they the colours you want?
Max: Yes . . . red, black, light blue and dark blue and green . . . and a watch. Black shoes. A feather.
Karl: Do you think you'd be able to find those things?
Max: I don't know.
Karl: . . . You're smiling, aren't you [in the drawing]?
Max: Mmm. And a bow-tie.
Karl: Have you ever seen anybody wearing that?
Max: No.

[Fairglen]

I am conscious here of Rosi Braidotti's warning that contemporary capitalism 'vampirises' new forms of difference. One could reasonably argue that these colourful, sideways imaginaries of communion clothing fall directly into the same consumerist trap that the Ikea commercial sets, cleverly inviting many Irish adults to link memories of their own childhoods to contemporary childhoods. However, there are two counterpoints to this. First, children do not have the same relative influence as adults in the child-focused marketplace. Second, the means of producing these special artefacts is a separate conversation – indeed, as Caoimhe's earlier reference to charity shops reminds us, borrowing and recycling clothes cannot be ruled out in this regard.

The previous section of this chapter indicated that it was not difficult for children in different settings to imagine and position themselves in relation to global icons. But engagement with the global metropolis and its pluralities was less evident. I have discussed elsewhere how, despite historically recent claims that Ireland's education sector does not know much about global diversity, there is often clear familiarity with pathologising tropes of the global racial other.[13] I reference this point in relation to another activity, which also asked children to respond to a video. The video asked similarly aged children in the US 'what does it mean to be hungry?' While global hunger was not specifically referenced in the film, it sparked an opportunity to consider the causes of hunger, and whether we could engage or move past pre-existing, westernised, individualist perspectives on this issue. This produced a zigzagging between scientific and religious meanings, ranging from global hunger to individual poverty, to the links between God's creation to human evolution.

Karl: What do you think about that [video]?
Alan: Sad.
Karl: Why?
Alan: Cause people like, people in Africa don't get food.
Karl: Right, did they mention Africa?
Alan and another: No.
Karl: . . . Ok, you were saying to me earlier on, God created the world, does anyone have an opinion why these things happen?
Child: Because they don't have money.

[Fairglen]

Again, despite the fact that starvation and global hunger was not mentioned, the notion of 'hunger' itself was affectively charged enough to trigger racialised tropes of the needy, unfortunate other, who has no money or resources for no apparent reason. It is notable that the word 'sad' is used above – this word appeared frequently in the context of articulating sadness for those experiencing exclusion and who are other. The clear challenge in terms of cultivating ethical accountability towards others here was in shifting limiting feelings of sympathy and sadness for an oversimplified other to engaging empathically with complex publics transnationally and translocally.

Examples of further possibilities and complexities in this area are articulated by Faith and Prabha, below. Faith described some of the freedoms that being a child, temporarily, in her grandmother's locality brought – being able to buy things yourself, not wearing any shoes. Prabha appeared to enjoy the same comforts in Ireland and in India – but regarded poverty in India and associated suffering ('some people cry') as a key difference.

Faith: Well, I had to live in a house with no roof . . . my Grandma didn't have any money to pay. They were building the house by themselves, they had to buy a lot of bricks, cement and everything.

Karl: Where? Zimbabwe?

Faith: Mmhmm. Most of it had the roof, and some of the bedrooms had the roof and the kitchen, and but the rest like the other places, didn't have any, like there's like a way at the back and at the front and there's another entrance over there.

Karl:	. . . What did you think of living there [for holidays]?
Faith:	Fun.
Karl:	What was your favourite part of it?
Faith:	We got to go to the shops by ourselves and buy lots of things.
Karl:	Like what?
Faith:	Like sweets and bread and everything.
Karl:	So that's the best part of living there?
Faith:	And we didn't have to wear any shoes.

As part of the same conversation about diasporic experience, Prabha, whose parents are Indian, stated:

Prabha:	. . . I like both places [Ireland and India].
Karl:	Do you like them for the same reasons or different reasons?
Prabha:	I like them for the same reasons.
Karl:	What are the reasons?
Prabha:	Because this place has TV, and that place has TV. This place is comfy, that place is comfy, in this place the internet is the same as that one, and everything is just the same.
Karl:	And what about the people?
Prabha:	Well the people are different.
Karl:	And how do you feel about that?
Prabha:	Well some people cry in my house, and they don't have any money. Some people try and get money but nobody gives them money.

[Raven Hill]

What Matters? Living a Good Life and Moral Judgement

Returning to chapter three's theme of bodies, one aspect of public policy making where there is significant moral consensus about 'good' childhoods is around promotion of healthy eating and physical activity to 'combat obesity'. Ireland has been part of the European Childhood Obesity Surveillance initiative since 2007, which monitors the risk of obesity. The major longitudinal study Growing Up in Ireland focuses on being overweight and obesity as key themes. Sarah Gillborn et al. describe discourses of fatness in UK childhood obesity policy as 'apocalyptic' in their assumption of the threat and burden of obesity, where certain (working-class, minority ethnic) bodies are constructed as more of a threat than others.[14] In Ireland, even supposedly effective community-oriented programmes such as 'Preparing for Life' (which offers antenatal education, home visits, and curriculum support) present middle-class norms (in terms of resources) for families to aspire to with regard to health and body weight.[15] As such the emphasis is on self and family transformation 'with support', in a way that ignores unjust, classed, racialised and gendered experiences of bodies. Hannah Jayne Bacon argues that the public, medical language of obesity is itself entangled with religious notions of sin, 'to construct a politics of choice that holds the dieter personally responsible for her fat'.[16]

The apocalyptic moralising of public health promotion discourse was something I was conscious of, given the ubiquity of health promotion in Ireland and, as such, in our encounters with schools. Health morality came up occasionally in our conversations, and children had some strong, but playful views on it.[17]

Karl:	If I was to ask you to tell me something that's healthy, would you be able to name something.
Orlaith:	Chocolate . . . well I'd say it is!
Anna:	Vegetables.
Karl:	. . . What about unhealthy food?
Naoise:	Chocolate, cake.
Orlaith:	Vegetables!
Yafa:	What happens when you eat unhealthy food?
Orlaith:	You get fat!
Anna:	You can't move . . . a pain in your tummy!
Karl:	What does a healthy person do?
Girls:	Run! Walk! Exercise!
Karl:	What about an unhealthy person?
Orlaith:	Sit and watch TV!
Karl:	Would you say you're healthy or unhealthy?
Orlaith:	Both . . . I eat chocolate and vegetables!
Naoise:	What's healthy and unhealthy at the exact same time is strawberries and chocolate!
Karl:	Do you ever see healthy or unhealthy people on TV?
Orlaith:	Yeah it's a programme, 'Secret Eaters' I think it's called.
Karl:	What's that about?
Orlaith:	It's when people, what their families, what other families eat, and they tell them to stop eating food.
Karl:	Why is it called 'Secret Eaters'?
Orlaith:	Cause they eat and they don't want to tell anybody . . . they don't want them to know.

[Fairglen]

As a domain where children can have some relative control over their bodies, food was an area of deep interest and engagement.

Children were highly capable of satirising prevailing moralities surrounding food and, as such, experiencing freedoms and relating to the world in ways that were not as available in other domains. The affirmative response to food as pleasurable above was infectious, while at the same time it was clear that the message they had heard/seen was that fatness was to be avoided, and that certain food practices (as portrayed in 'Secret Eaters') were shameful. Orlaith's view that she was both 'healthy and unhealthy' here was creative in its disregard of binary ideas.

The final video-response activity we engaged in involved two short time-lapse pieces. One showed a dandelion flower bloom, die and transform into a seed head. The other was a time-lapse video of a boy growing from early childhood to adolescence, captured by his father on a daily basis. Both this video and the 'White Dress' short film facilitated discussions about living a good life, death, and whether humans exist on either side of birth (that is, whether they have a soul or spirit). Many were enthusiastic about discussing the notion of a soul, transcendent moral judgement and what happens, if anything, after death. All of the children in both excerpts below identified with particular religious traditions and/or communities, and a number deviated from doctrine in their views. Conor, Grace, Eric and Chris identified with Christianity (Catholicism, Christian Orthodox and Methodism) and Tariq, Majid and Ismail with Islam (denominations unknown).

Karl: Do you think the girl in the video has a soul?
Conor: A soul is like if you have a soul you're good and if you don't have a soul you're very bad.
Karl: Do you think she has a soul?

Conor: No . . . because she stole. People with souls don't
            steal.

Adam: Yes, she does have a soul, cause everybody has a
            soul. And the only way you're good is if the soul is
            burning. If it's not it means you're not good.

Karl: Do you think people have souls or a spirit?

Tariq: No.

Karl: Grace, what do you think?

Grace: Yeah . . . inside them.

Faith: I think everyone has them . . . in their heart.

Eric: Your soul is also called your spirit. And everyone,
            even if you're bad, of course you have a spirit cause
            your spirit keeps you alive.

Karl: Where do you think it is?

Eric: It's all over your body and inside you . . . cause
            when you die your spirit will go up to God and you'll
            be alive in heaven . . . when your body's buried, God
            will scan you or something and get a replacement of
            your body and then when your spirit goes up it will
            go into the same body and you'll be alive in heaven.

Conor: And the best thing about heaven is . . . you live for
            ever.

Chris: And if you don't have enough blood in your body
            you'll die, cause blood is the strongest thing in your
            body.

Ismail: There's something on your shoulder, like a ghost,
            and if you do something bad . . . then when you go
            to heaven, it sees how much good things and bad
            things [you did].

[Raven Hill]

Both of the preceding excerpts on healthy eating and on the soul demonstrate the range of religious, spiritual, and scientific discourses – moral and otherwise – that the children zigzagged between in their encounters with us, with one another and with ideas. These conversations illustrate the plurality of children's worldviews, in a way that exemplifies them as interdependent minorities rather than 'just children', 'just Catholics' or 'just Muslims'. At the same time, they demonstrate the pull of the desire to make absolute truth claims before those categorised as other. The final conversation excerpt brings us full circle in terms of one of the key themes noted at the beginning of the book: the fusion of consumption and religiosity as part of children's material cultural experience. Children's sense-making around morality involves being part of multiple relationships – in this case, with parents, Allah, angels and Spongebob Squarepants.

Karl:	Majid, who would make the rules about right and wrong?
Majid:	Mm, the judge?
Karl:	Is there anyone else? Who tells you what's right and wrong?
Majid:	My Daddy and my Mommy.
Karl:	And does God have anything to do with it?
Majid:	Em, yes.
Karl:	Would you say God, or Allah?
Majid:	Allah . . . well mostly Allah does, and the angels see if it's right or wrong, they're on your shoulder, and they write down what's bad or good.
Yafa:	So, Majid, when I steal something, who tells me it's wrong?

Majid: . . . A devil?

Karl: Does he [devil] do good things or bad things?

Majid: Bad.

Karl: And would the devil tell me to steal? [yes] And who tells me not to steal?

Majid: Angel?

Karl: And where are the angels?

Majid: Eh, here [points to his shoulder].

Karl: Where did you see that?

Majid: Em, Spongebob?

[Raven Hill]

Conclusion

This chapter has examined children's ethics from a critical postsecular perspective. The analysis was premised on what Rosi Braidotti refers to as the nomadic nature of ethics. Nomadic ethical agency centralises encounters and world-making over individual conforming to predefined, absolute values or ideas regarding the good and the bad and what affinities one should hold/be capable of. 'What matters' here is matter: world-making, and the cultivation and experience of plural encounters through material human and non-human culture. The experience of what matters is embodied and located in specific places and settings which are connected to secular–religious negotiations and contestations on larger scales (nation, globe). The singular encounters documented here partially illustrate children's negotiation of religious, classed, gendered, racialised and other experiences and norms, and the forms of accountability and affinity that are imagined, enacted, claimed and refuted in the process. For example, Mairead imagined a relationship with the church space and, indirectly, with clergy, based on movement, where fun and holiness were not mutually exclusive. Grace in certain ways eschewed or downplayed accountability to her multi-ethnic peer group, while at the same time demanding that her Catholic educators be accountable to her in explaining the afterlife.

Mappings and the conversations that ensued from our activities enabled the examination of different modes and rhythms of life (living together, praying in different places and ways) which allowed greater visibility of certain children's experiences. Mappings also 'took flight' in different ways, zigzagging between the intimate, private space of the home, phallocentric global monuments/icons and local structures, raising complex, unanswered questions about what and who they have affinities with. Encounters with videos and ensuing discussions demonstrated engagement and disengagement with plurality in terms of further affinities, and enactments and refutations of accountability towards particular others. For example, the 'Abbi's Circle' video sparked questions about the boundaries of 'sounding Irish' in one context with certain children, while, in another, it raised concerns about immigration control and injustice for certain others. Racialised sympathy for, and the assumed foreignness of, specific 'global' others was articulated but could arguably be complicated by engagement with more complex narratives and sharing of affinities and empathies. The discussion of these themes, and not least the question of living a good life and moral judgement, illustrated children's interdependencies and shared vulnerabilities as they simultaneously articulated and departed from religious, scientific and reason-based absolutes.

Chapters three and four have presented the book's critical postsecular perspective on the child as plural. They do not simply progress or fail to progress through a linear series of socio-religious developmental stages towards reproducing societal norms. They may grow sideways and find creative ways to mediate and contest them. Drawing on Rosi Braidotti, focusing on our nomadic ethical agency centralises encounters, over individual conforming to predefined notions of good and bad and what affinities one should hold. From a critical postsecular perspective, we must regard children's nuanced experiences of secular–religious relations and their dynamic ethical encounters as public, political and educational concerns. This requires understanding that children encounter the world in ways that may seek to reproduce it and may not. In order to find some accommodation in an unjust system, they may grow sideways to have encounters with persons, objects, images, ideas and places that may ordinarily be cast as something they are not capable of.

Part of the becoming public of school systems and the building of ethical relations requires us to acknowledge not just present-day childhoods, but also the variety of past memories and future imaginaries of childhood that insist alongside and in our everyday experience of, and views on, schooling. The final empirical chapter speaks to the need to explore collective memories, with a view to supporting adults to grow sideways too, and to find new or alternative ways of engaging with past images and future imaginaries of childhood. Chapter five thus re-engages with parents and with a wider array of adults' views on childhood, education, and religion. This includes, school staff, clergy and senior citizens who were interviewed in the four key localities noted in chapter two.

5

Remembering Childhood, Engaging Ghosts, Imagining School Futures

Introduction

Collective childhood sensory and material culture, family rhythms, worldly and transcendent goals, social obligations, and wider public and policy discourses have a significant role to play in the maintenance and change of unjust school and societal cultures. This chapter focuses primarily on adults' images of the past and, more specifically, on images of childhood, religion and schooling. Drawing largely on interviews with white, settled, Irish adults (school staff, parents, clergy and senior citizens) who were raised within the Catholic Church in Ireland, it sheds light on how collective memory feeds into socio-religious continuity and change, and how collective experience and feeling, rather than rational choice, alone inform adults' worldviews and their orientations towards, and future imaginings of, childhood.

The policy promise of a school system that guarantees freedom through the power of individual/familial choice is persuasive. Using the cover of modernist discourses of childhoods based on rights, this promise frames education, and growing up in Ireland, as being on a progressive, secularising historical path. But in reality, apparent progress along a particular path under neoliberalism requires a significant amount of forgetting and collective reinterpretation. 'We', in more uncertain risk societies[1] are incited to cast off collective solidarities, wonder, (inter)dependency and experiences of pain and construct individual choice biographies which mitigate uncertainties for ourselves and for our children's futures. But adults' complex relationships to past experience challenge prevailing individualist notions of religious/non-religious choice and rationality. They also demonstrate that adults never leave childhood states and certain ghosts behind; they learn to live with them. In the context of the ongoing institutionalisation and pain of particular communities (including asylum seekers and Travellers), I argue in this chapter that we need to support adults 'growing sideways' and making lateral connections between past, present and future generations of childhood as an ethical issue. Growing sideways, for adults, means raising historical consciousness and enacting 'accountability for the transnational places we all inhabit in late post-modernity'.[2]

Certainly, any process of imagining child futures is multifaceted. As the data analysis shows, adult participants viewed past and present childhoods, and their children's future trajectories, through a mix of lenses noted in chapter one: moral discipline, psychological development, rights and appropriate participation. Individualised, racialised, classed and gendered religious and non-religious interests underpinned these lenses, in a way that posed significant challenges to engagement with plurality. In particular, participants' attachment to specific kinds of 'past' institutionalised violence (for example, of corporal punishment, physical abuse) meant the pain/fear that present-day institutions (schools, media, Direct Provision, etc.) inflict on specific populations were less recognised. If Irish society continues to fail to see links between institutionalised pain and fear in the past and present as a feature of racialised, capitalist modernity, it will continue to be haunted. However, as quoted with reference to Avery Gordon's work in chapter one, a ghost can also represent 'a future possibility, a hope . . . we must reckon with it graciously, attempting to offer it a hospitable memory out of a concern for justice'.[3]

Collective memory: Some caveats

Coser, and Halbwachs outline certain distinguishing features of collective memory. It involves a distinct set of memories and common experiences drawn from a relatively coherent body of people, developed over a long period of time.[4] There are as many collective memories as there are social groups, for example, Catholics, working classes, women, sports teams, etc. While it is individual persons who remember, those individuals are situated in a specific group context, which is drawn upon to narrate the past. Our experience of the past is thus always a relative reconstruction, shaped to some degree by present concerns. Remembering is also laden with ethical challenges, since it offers the possibility of common identification with or disidentification with others, and inclusive and exclusionary forgettings and imaginings of the future.[5]

Four caveats are important in considering the analysis that follows. First, it does not seek to displace the direct experiences and voices of children with adults' reminiscences of 'lost landscapes' of childhood.[6] This point is particularly significant, given the adult-centred lens through which we look at childhood – and the otherness of childhood that adults can never directly access. Second, I do not assume that adults' present experiences and orientations entirely frame, or are determined by, their childhood memories. As Coser notes, Schwartz argues that 'the past is always a compound of persistence and change, of continuity and newness'.[7] Third, and accordingly, I do not assume that participants' memories of childhood are the entire basis of their adult identities or educational desires for children.[8] Fourth, certainly, any given childhood event or experience can have multiple different interpretations in/after the moment and later. Indeed, the very fact that 'good' childhoods can be and are contested is regarded here as an important way of thinking about and confronting unjust secular–religious formations in schooling. Irish and international histories of clerical abuse underline the importance of such reconstructions for women, children, minority ethnic, LGBT and other groups who were systematically victimised and typically forced to internalise their oppression.[9]

Fear, Wonder, Piety and Pain: Material Culture and Acting Rational?

As discussed in chapter one, modern societal efforts to construct an ideal, precious, yet appropriately participating, uncomplicated child figure that is distant from adulthood 'does not fit children – doesn't fit the pleasures and terrors we recall'.[10] There was a clear acknowledgement of terror – or at least fear – in childhoods *past* in the data. Those who were roughly aged forty years plus were far more likely to report a childhood fear of clerical authority and experiences of harsh school discipline. Unsurprisingly, some felt that religious meaning was inaccessible to them in childhood. Liam and Fiona, below, both felt that the degree of rote learning in their religious instruction was oppressive and largely meaningless. But Liam and Valerie, both Catholic school principals, sought to highlight their view that participation is now central to education:

> In primary it was very much rote learning, the catechism, learning things off by heart and also [I] hadn't a clue what it meant . . . but simply that was it and you had to learn it. And there was a certain fear involved and if you didn't learn it . . . there was a threat of being hit and so it was under a fear thing, that's why education is gone full circle. Children love coming to school, they love learning, they're open to learning.
>
> [Liam, Principal, Scoil Cholmcille]

> I remember the punishments were like taking away conduct marks and if you got three black marks you were sent to the nun down to the office. There was the fright of having canes and being hit . . . Some days, you will be over (in the church) every day for a month or two trying to practise all of the songs, services . . . I don't really remember knowing why we were making communion . . . I have no recollection of the lessons that went with it, and your understanding into what was happening.
>
> [Fiona, teacher and parent, Catholic, Raven Hill]

> I was always very young from my class, and that time you couldn't make your communion unless you were seven,

> so I made my communion in second [class/grade] with everyone else made it in first [class] . . . We used have to go back every day to first class for Religion, and I remember being kind of, feeling awkward about that . . . I remember the day clearly of getting their hair done and I was the eldest girl in my family . . . you [were] afraid to put a foot wrong in a sense. It's not that kind of thing we promote now, that there was no sense of any relationship with God, anything like that, it was just learning your prayers, and doing the right thing at the right time.
>
> [Valerie, Principal, Fairglen]

Visceral recollections of not just fear and pain, but piety and wonder are outlined below, with different implications for how each person remembered childhood and schooling. Sarah, a local resident of Fairglen in her seventies, was one of the few participants to acknowledge that, as has been well documented by Moira Maguire amongst others,[11] punishment was not evenly distributed to all children and families in the past. Poor, working-class and Traveller families bore the brunt of parent–child separation and institutionalisation. Both Rachel and Sarah (below) saw the use of fear as a way to maintain control as one of the reasons they left the Catholic Church, while other adults (including Fr Diarmuid) indicated the view that fear may have done them some good.

> If [Catholics] had any doubts, anything like that, they couldn't really talk about that, in *my* view as a child. Because we never heard of anybody not believing in anything or if anybody did they would be scorned, even by your parents, to some extent. I suppose I had *felt* abuse in a way at school, not for myself so much, but for the other

175

children . . . my father . . . rented a little shop in the city and he worked a lot for the religious . . . Everybody else had no money . . . So I felt when I was at school that the nuns knew that, and I think if they knew your parents and respected your parents, you were likely to be safe . . . there were very unfortunate children in my school who came from huge families . . . They were slapped and slapped and slapped . . . I didn't really know about the terrible abuse at all when I kind of started feeling I wanted something else for [my] children . . . we felt, for the children, we had to sort our thinking out, and I started looking at other religions, long before I came across Bahá'í.

[Sarah, Fairglen resident, Bahá'í]

I had a real sense of 'this is something really sacred and holy, receiving the body of Jesus'. I didn't know what it meant . . . how can you explain the sacredness of something, either, to an eight-year-old when it's a difficult concept for adults to understand? They get it that it's something very holy and special. But they only really get it if it is part of a regular practice . . . I was in hospital a few weeks before my first communion. The only time I've ever been in hospital in my life . . . Sister Agnes . . . used to come in every day to teach me my prayers and to make sure I didn't fall behind. So at the time I didn't really appreciate the nun coming in terrorising me in school, or in hospital, but I did appreciate it afterwards.

[Fr Diarmuid, Curate of a suburban setting]

At Mass, mostly what I was doing was concentrating on what I was supposed to be saying, what I was supposed to be doing . . . or else I'd get a slap. To be fair I was pretty devoted when I was younger . . . I think that we put a higher value on the actual religious side of it in my time . . . Not that we understood *better*, that's not true, they do understand what they're doing now. I think the difference was that at *home* our parents would have talked to us more about the actual event itself. Whereas now generally they seem to be talking more about getting the clothes, the party afterwards, the dinner, getting the money, cards, who's going to come and see me in my outfit, that kind of stuff.

[Rachel, teacher, agnostic/raised Catholic, Scoil Cholmcille]

A concern for contemporary children's meaningful individual participation was evident throughout adults' accounts, as a present-day foil to these collective memories of fear, devotion and wonder. However, despite these commonalities, different visions of a 'good' childhood overlapped in the memories and current views of participants: from the perceived need for moral discipline, to psychological concern for child-centred investment and wellbeing, to the encouragement of appropriate, individual, active child participation.[12] For example, Fr Diarmuid's and Rachel's accounts above, while contesting how well children understand first communion, emphasised the need for rehearsed institutional adult guidance in order for children to *best* understand religious meaning. Elsewhere, Father Tomás showed great affection for the children he worked with and encouraged greater informality and participation in first communion preparation. However, he viewed that participation in somewhat instrumental terms, and as a means of repairing or deepening their parents' relationships with the Church.

The more you involve children . . . if you put a child on stage you fill a hall, I think if you get children involved in preparation for Mass, and get them working, say, then parents will come along, and again, they begin to see the value of something they have lost, they can come back to kind of realising that there, there is something there that you can hang on to if you like, or that can give you comfort or strength or whatever, and maybe that's one of the things the Church has lost out, possibly, that ability to reach out to people . . . When I was a child we had a shop, post office and bar. The priest would call regularly, he would have the dinner or the supper. Very often when we saw the priests, we ran. If you saw the teacher or the guard, you jumped the ditch. The big change I have found, youngsters are much more at ease and able to chat or whatever. I said to a child another day, she said 'I'm reading a prayer of the faithful at Mass', and I said 'you have never read before' and she said, 'you must be deaf' . . . Parents say 'oh, you can't say that', but I love [that] they can be themselves.

[Fr Tomás, Fairglen]

The pattern the data reveals thus far is how fear was seen as common to most Catholic childhoods in what was, for many, a systematically oppressive society. Despite many school and religious leaders' awareness of differences in families' socio-economic status, however, there was a view amongst most participants that fear, anxiety and oppression in children's socio-religious experience had been left behind. As alluded to in earlier chapters, the perception of children's lives and participation was very much tied to Catholic-centric, classed, racialised and gendered types of judgement regarding certain children and families, often erasing children's pain in the present.

National progress for all? The ghosts of children's pain in the present

The 'need' for institutional guidance to control appropriate child and family participation in sacraments expressed above was as implicitly classed, racialised and gendered as it was a concern for the sacredness of the sacrament. Sometimes it was explicitly prejudiced. For example, Fr Gerard separately described the large first communion ceremonies he conducted in his parish as 'a nightmare', because of some families who are 'purely there for the day out . . . in the biggest dresses, in the biggest suits and the least interest in what was going on'. He later alluded to poor and Traveller families in this regard. At times, casually racist urban and folk myths were offered regarding first communion and Mass participation without any clear point other than to underline the perceived otherness of Travellers as exaggeratedly, irrationally religious and materialistic. Eimear, who taught in Fairglen, stated:

Eimear: The only difference now, I feel now there is more competition. I remember doing my communion, I was looking at other dresses, but I don't think my parents were, it was myself rather than my parents, I think parents these days are competitive . . . I taught in [regional town], there would be a high Travelling [sic] community there . . . they are the most religious people I have ever met, and this poor girl lost her mother . . . everyone got a Mass card and the father came in saying would we pray for the child and the mother, and even the communion – this story shocked me – a boy in my class, his sister was doing her communion, he had the pink suit, the

179

fake tan and they had [celebrity] Jordan's carriage that she was married in, then she had this tiara that said 'hallelujah' with crystals, and when she made her communion, click went the switch and hallelujah started flashing all the way down.

Karl: Did you witness this?

Eimear: No, one of the teachers was at it and passed on the story. I don't know if it's exaggerated but I feel like it's not [laughter], it's just another different community.

[Fairglen]

The above children's and families' religiosity was regarded as somewhat abnormal, an inappropriate form of participation in a largely settled, culturally Catholic context. Despite Eimear's recognition that 'the only difference' between when she made communion and today 'is more competition', she drew on remote control tiaras and celebrity carriages as symbols to present Traveller families and children as failing to present gendered Catholic child innocence. Garry and Laura, both members of the Traveller community, provided a counterstory, or contesting narrative, which bore witness to the continuity of social exclusion for Travellers.[13] They also stated the simple fact that, while many in the Traveller community identify with and practise Catholicism, a diversity of worldviews exists amongst Travellers.

Garry: I was never a very religious person, even now I'm not, but I remember having the Angelus at six o'clock every evening, being kicked to Mass and if I didn't go [my mother would] . . . find out I didn't go . . . I have a son, and he is a bit ultra [religious], he goes to Knock [Catholic holy shrine and pilgrimage site] every fortnight. I mean I cannot understand that kind of ultra-religious, he didn't get that from me.

Laura: . . . The Catholic Church was very much involved with Travellers, but there was a positive and negative. That stigma's still there today, and I think the ways families are looking negatively at priests today is because of publicity, because of media.

Garry: But I suppose that negative side would have been there in the past as well. If some clergy or religious order had seen Travellers in an area [they] would right away think they're there for no good reason, you know? There was a suspicion there that wasn't put on other communities.

Laura: . . . I do believe though in this day and age that there should be more interaction with the Catholic Church and Travellers. But I do feel a lot of Travellers moving away from the Church because of publicity [regarding abuse].

For both Garry and Laura, the issue of Travellers' continued exclusion was not simply related to distrust of the Church due to clerical abuse. The specific negative impact that racist media and public political stigma had and has on Travellers, particularly in institutions, is an ongoing concern. Fear in childhood was viewed by the majority of (white, settled, middle-class) participants as something that was not an issue contemporarily. Garry and Laura's comments were amongst the few to explicitly contest the notion of universal progress in relation to religion, society and childhood, and to demonstrate the wider disproportionate burdens and stigma placed on marginalised families.

This focus on fear as being something of the past, and something to avoid, additionally meant that the minor pleasures of engaging fear fictively were not a significant area of exploration.[14] Discourses of childhood innocence, *appropriate* participation and of generational order – which presents children as in need of adult protection, both from risky adults on the one hand and excessive 'adult-like' pleasure derived from material culture on the other – was a common thread across most of the data above. These themes aligned with public discourses and policy efforts across a variety of domains (health, religion, school) to responsibilise unequally positioned families and children to work on themselves and make the right choices while failing to consider how diverse (Catholic) populations pursue their religiosity.

Material culture: Religious/ritual pleasures and contesting 'good' childhoods

Memory is not statically stored in individual heads. Rather, it is materialised, distributed and sustained through encounters with bodies, objects, places, rituals and the potentially uncategorisable, pre-verbal sensations (smell, sight, sound, taste, touch, tempo) we perceive in those encounters. Material objects, places and family and social rhythms, was one medium through which participants recalled/re-experienced Catholic religious ritual. Significant and special embodied/sensory and cultural experiences described below include dressing in special clothes, eating, praying, fasting, marching in procession, taking photographs, and playing at receiving the eucharist.

I don't really like the limelight . . . but I liked dressing up and I wore my older sister's dress, because back then

182

everybody wore hand-me-downs. Went for a nice meal with my family afterwards . . . I remember learning lots of prayers, and I was given the responsibility of reading the first reading and very proud of it. I love singing so I was delighted with all of that. I felt the community as well got involved, even neighbours . . . they would come to watch it, and afterwards they'd all come over and congratulate you, especially the Corpus Christi procession . . . coming with baskets of petals to give me to take part in the procession . . . I think I had a veil, and I had a bag, and I got a lovely prayer book I remember, and I loved it and I kept it, the pictures in it were beautiful and I always brought it to Mass and I couldn't understand why it didn't follow the Mass, and I was very cross that it wasn't following.

[Aoife, learning support teacher, Scoil Cholmcille]

I remember practising with pieces of wafer, going down to the church, and I remember even getting excited about the wafer, even the priest gives us unblessed pieces of bread to practise with.

[Sinead, teacher, Fairglen]

I remember mine like yesterday . . . there was this lovely dress in the window, my mother and father got the veil, and the umbrella (parasol) and everything . . . then I had my communion, we were practising with the school and all that. Then we just went for a family meal afterwards . . . I have little cousins that are [live a settled life], they have their hair fixed lovely and flowy dresses . . . they look like children. I think [Travellers today are] just living up to everyone's expectations.

[Danielle, young Traveller woman]

Julie: I still have my holy picture at home in my kitchen and I talk to [it] on a regular basis [chuckles].

Karl: Who's the picture of?

Julie: Oh Jesus himself [laughs] . . . I came from a big family, very little money, there were poor days . . . Prayer was a very big thing and, by God, you certainly didn't go against your parents, because . . . you weren't just afraid of them, we grew up at the time of the devil, and the big red fire was there. And I don't know, I don't think it done us [harm].

Therese: I think it's so wrong, purgatory, that part of religion . . . Kids making their communion are not told anything about the devil and burning. We were brought up with that.

[Julie and Therese, special needs assistants,
Scoil Cholmcille]

Sinead's excitement about receiving first eucharist resonates with Ridgely Bale's US research, which argues that sensory experience is a significant and underappreciated element of Catholic children's experience of the sacred. Julie expressed an embodied experience of religiosity that was directly tied to a material object. But an interesting aspect of these and other adults' accounts is an unconscious forgetting, a lack of explicit attention to the history and significance of consumption and material culture in the performance of religious ritual. Lisa Godson argues that the nineteenth-century devotional revolution was 'nothing short of a consumer revolution', given the scale of consumption of imported European religious objects which moved Catholics away from local devotion and towards the institutional Church.[15] Internationally, 'non-ecclesial' material culture has been part of first communion ceremonies since at least the eighteenth century.[16] As such, the mixing of religious and non-religious symbols and practices stretches much further back than contemporary moral panics regarding the materialism of certain first communion ceremonies. Nevertheless, the material culture of childhood and first communion was carefully discussed in a way that avoided representation of one's own childhood as 'excessive'.

It was clear in at least two ways that most participants viewed 'good' contemporary childhoods through a primarily rational, psychological-developmentalist rather than a spiritual/religious lens channelled through material culture. First, when disciplining their children, parents rarely referenced a transcendent goal or figure (such as heaven or God). This was perhaps in an effort to avoid reproducing past collective experiences of fear and sinfulness. Second, the Christian notion of children being closer to God was infrequently expressed. This rationalist presentation of the child tended to neglect the role that material culture plays in children's lives. One exception was Sr Ruth, who was in her late eighties and presented the following story about a child from her own locality. While regarding children as having an innocent, essential, spiritual curiosity, she framed the girl's story below in terms of wonder, mystery, religious material culture (a picture of an angel). She also critiqued modern adult guidance and the generational moral order.

> Strangely, children absorb so much that is spiritual . . . a little lady now at home, a four-year-old . . . the teacher explained the prayer to the Angel Guardian to [her class], and home she came, she wanted an angel . . . so they rang me and said they, could you get an angel of some sort for her, even a picture of an angel . . . and I sent it, and no way does she go to bed at night without kneeling down

and saying her prayers to the Angel Guardian. You see, it shows it's actually *in* children, the spirituality is there, all it needs is to be encouraged . . . it is from the adult they pick up something that isn't spiritual afterwards.

[Sr Ruth, regional town]

But Sr Ruth was relatively unique, and there appeared to be little language with which to talk about contemporary material culture beyond consumerist/religious binaries. Separately, the contemporary pace, scale and wastefulness of consumerist material culture and its disruptive influence was a concern for some. Below, Hannah, who was in her seventies, ran a family business in rural Fairglen for much of her life. She strongly praised local Catholic priests, who led the historic economic, social and cultural development (or 'civilising') of the rural community. Her critique of present-day social relations was not of consumerism's existence, but of its speed and its pressures.

Hannah: Look at all the shops, and the ways of money, and you must have all the fashions. That's what's killing the people like. My first communion dress, then, it was given to another girl the following year, she was an only girl. My mother gave it to her and her mother gave it on to someone else the following year and it went on the whole time . . . now there are too many choices . . . Things are too fast.

Karl: . . . What gives you a sense of community . . . even if it has changed?

Hannah: The older people, they are fine, you should be asking the young people what keeps them together. I think so. We won't change now.

[Fairglen]

Hannah also referenced meeting an Australian priest who confirmed her view that the changing of Mass timing, for example, to Saturday night, had been 'detrimental' to Catholic observance. While everyone interviewed had to adjust to changing socio-religious rhythms, Hannah's words indicate the experience of feeling temporally displaced in her own locality, or, as Janssen refers to it, 'distimed'.[17] Factors in the wider experience of temporal displacement included the rapid pace of the contemporary, the deinstitutionalisation of Catholic identity and the diversification of family rhythms and forms. As discussed below, alongside changing material culture, changing family mobilities and rhythms have also led to contrasting views regarding the role of the school in religious education – with the family coming into view for some as needing to play a more active role in 'reproducing' faith.

Changing Socio-Religious Rhythms and Future Imaginaries

The accounts from Catholic school staff earlier in this chapter gave further insight into the collective embodied experience of our largely white, female and Catholic-heritage primary-teaching population.[18] They also indicated the rhythm and sheer scale of preparation for sacramental events that they are responsible for maintaining, an issue which caused some frustration for some. Gráinne's (below) school was located in an area where a vote was being carried out by the Department of Education and Skills. The vote was to find out the kind of school that pre-school parents preferred, in order to assess if divestment of a Catholic school in the area to another patron was realistic. All of the primary schools in the town were Christian and all but one had a Catholic ethos. In many ways encapsulating the increasingly normalised promotion of the Catholic school, and the responsibilisation of individual families to 'choose' appropriately, Gráinne stated:

> Our school is going down the line of that we are going to keep our Roman Catholic ethos, [the principal] Liam has been pushing it. Any time that our school is advertised now it really is 'the Roman Catholic school', like as Beth said that's what we are. So if you don't want your child to be receiving holy communion, that's your decision, it's very annoying, every year . . . I've had three or four that haven't been receiving [communion], that's great, that's their choice, just don't come to us because it is very frustrating . . . [If first communion was prepared for] outside school, yeah it would take a lot of pressure off us. But it will be really interesting to see how they will do that, because they wouldn't be getting commitment, the numbers will fall, but maybe [they] should.
>
> [Gráinne, teacher, Scoil Cholmcille]

On the other side of the school gates, as it were, parents Helen and Maria in Fairglen had a different view of sacramental preparation and the decline in Catholic devotion, somewhat akin to their parish priest, Father Tomás. Rather than suggest that their faith was declining, they felt the challenge of family religious commitments lay in how busy and complex family life was. They still viewed sacramental preparation as having 'a better structure if it's done in the school'. They admitted that broader familial commitment to first communion might 'fall off' if consigned to after-school classes. However, Helen, unprompted, referred to the fact that parents in their school choose to *trust* the parish priest in the context of sacramental preparation. While, in one sense, they contested public (political and religious) discourses which over-responsibilise families, they also relied upon risk society discourses, of choosing to place one's trust in a potentially risky institution for children, and did not tend to examine collective support for, or changing forms of, the parish structure.

Helen: Father Stephen is grateful to us that we trust him with our children. It makes an awful difference.

Maria: . . . Out of school, parents work . . . they might have other children, they might have 100 million things going on and I think kids might lose out [if sacramental preparation was conducted outside of school].

[Fairglen]

Clare Holdsworth, writing about Urry's work on mobilities, argues that 'the geographical dispersal of family and friends means that we cannot rely on . . . frequent and chance encounters to maintain intimate and family relations'.[19] In other words, these encounters must be planned. Events such as first communion are dependent on the structuring of childhood in primary schools across Ireland and provide a way of both retaining a more or less strong familial affiliation to a Catholic heritage and of allowing families to get together. Their material cultural expression, while often downplayed and distinctly classed, racialised and gendered, was also a key part of maintaining that majoritarian (local, national) sense of 'us'. Ríona felt Catholic in name only, and linked to religious tradition through her parents. Interestingly, she further tied this cultural legacy to Irishness in the context of an ethno-nationally and religiously mixed parent group interview.

Ríona: I suppose we are both Catholic, but only just by default because we were Irish and our families are Catholic, but we haven't still fully decided whether we're going to have [our five-year-old son] make his communion and do those things or not . . . I think my parents would be very disappointed if the kids didn't make their communion, so that would probably be the biggest thing that still has us discussing it.

Yafa: So you would probably just consider doing it?

Ríona: Just to keep them happy . . . Good old Irish guilt!

[St Michael's]

Given the politics of suburban place outlined in chapters one and two, some Catholic parents who were actively working with the Church had to adjust to or create alternative conceptual frameworks and rhythms beyond Catholic schooling for sacramental preparation, and their children's schooling more broadly. Nicole was brought up Catholic in a working-class suburb in a high-rise flat. Unusually for the 1970s, her adopted father, from infancy, was a North African Muslim man. He and her mother married with the understanding that her 'Mam kept up the Catholic background' in the household – a maternal Catholicism which Nicole actively sought to reproduce. Having been turned off by the elitist 'vibe' of a Catholic school in the area, Nicole had no idea what the alternative Educate Together school involved – not least in relation to religious education. But she became centrally involved in supporting Catholic after-school classes in the school building.

Nicole: I was sayin' if [my daughter] goes to the school, how are we goin' to practise the Catholic? [*sic*] . . . I was asking a few Mammies 'what's the kids doin' here that are Catholic like?' And Grace [from the Parents' Association] was like 'ah we have a Catholic class running and we only set it up' . . . that's when I enrolled me child in.

Karl: We've skipped [in the interview] from you not going to Mass to being involved in the Catholic parents' (after-school association), so what's the gap there?

Nicole: Well I always – didn't go to Mass [*sic*] but I was always very religious at home. Like, I do, like do prayers here all the time, I'm always talking to [my children] that there's a Heaven up there . . . I'll always say 'I'm a Catholic and I don't believe in hell, and whether you're a good person or a bad person God is gonna to open the gate to you no matter what' . . . So when we went to the Educate Together then obviously we had to start going back to Mass.

Yafa: And why is it 'obviously' we had to go to Mass?

Nicole: Because of the gap as well . . . I wanted her to be more involved, let her think it was more important that she was going to these classes . . . makin' it more believable that you go to God's house and you teach in school about God and stuff like that.

[Raven Hill]

Nicole's words indicate the new formulation of a community of 'Mammies' who support their children's religious formation outside of school hours. While the labour of (re)producing familial worldviews was gendered, this example, and those of parents and children from minority communities in chapters two and three, indicate how collective solidarities form or continue to maintain pockets of religious practice.

Worldviews and school futures

Alexander argues that the paradox of moral education is that:

> to teach the exercise of free choice requires limiting freedom of choice . . . it does not follow, however, that all instructional intentions are equally desirable, that inculcation of every faith commitment is morally equivalent to every other.[20]

Alexander contends that the key question is whether the intention is 'to eventually empower or emasculate the youngster'. The gendered terminology of 'emasculation' is problematic, but the point remains from chapters one to three: it is not possible, whether through secular or religious schools, to provide children with a neutral menu of options. The paradox of providing religious education that claims to support children to (a) ultimately form their own view and/or (b) engage with plurality was clear in the data.

> I would be religious in my views definitely, if I was ever upset I would say my prayers . . . my grandmother would be very religious and I think it came from her . . . It's important to provide the Catholic ethos to the children. When they come to an age, then they can make their own decision . . . but you can't make a decision on something if you haven't experienced it . . . I personally prefer how Educate Together go about religion because they do have a strong emphasis

on every religion . . . I always love listening to [my niece] because there is such a worldly approach . . . they have so many different religions and so many religious cultures.

[Eimear, teacher, Fairglen]

Every child thinks Mass is boring, but I say if you listen to what they're saying, there's a story every time you go. I think as they get a bit older, maybe pay more attention to it, they'll get more from it. But my oldest son, by the time he gets to confirmation he reckons he's going to be finished going to Mass at that stage like. He doesn't know that I'm going to keep him going [chuckles]! . . . I was brought up with [religion], and I think a little bit of moral guidance outside the home isn't a bad thing to have. And in life they're going to meet people who are very religious and some people who just aren't.

[Geraldine, parent, Scoil Cholmcille]

My attitude is I want our kids to be brought up with religion and make an educated choice later on in life. If they don't want to follow the same path, they have the education behind them, they can decide I don't want to, where if you bring them up with no religion then it's very hard for them to find religion . . . personally I would send my child to an Educate Together school [if the choice was there] . . . because they get religion from us at home, they don't need it to be pushed on them inside in school.

[Darren, parent, Catholic, Grange
Church of Ireland school]

Like the majority of Catholic participants, none of the above attended Mass regularly, but they felt a personal, spiritual relationship with God and saw Catholic religious instruction as being morally and/or socially important. This pattern is unsurprising, as, as noted in chapter one, Pew's 2018 research reported that 92 per cent of non-practising Christians in Ireland were raising their children as Christians. Understandably, then, there were different views regarding where and when faith formation should take place. Unlike Helen and Maria (earlier), who wished to see religious instruction continue during school, a number felt the Educate Together model of teaching about multiple religions (as part of a wider ethical curriculum), with religious instruction after school, was more desirable. This aligned with the views of two different parents in Raven Hill: Mark (below), who was raised Catholic but was non-religious, and Maita, who was Zimbabwean and had a strong Methodist devotion.

Mark: The fact that it was an Educate Together really sealed the deal for us . . . the fact that a child wouldn't be forced into religion to make the communion, to say prayers, that kind of stuff . . . we have absolutely no problem with his eyes being opened up to other cultures and other religions and my wife and myself have said if he turned round when he is ten or twelve years and said 'I fancy this religion', then ok, we will support him as much as we can. We didn't want to do what had been done to us and had it basically rammed down our throats.

Karl: Would you prefer there to be more Educate Together schools or would you prefer more at Catholic schools or, what would your ideal school be like living here?

Maita: . . . It's a tough question, I would prefer a Christian type of – maybe if it is being taught in schools like Christianity but then . . . some people are not Christians – maybe if we could say Educate Together.

Yafa: . . . Religion [that is, faith formation] is not taught in Educate Together schools. Do you offer your child religion class outside of school?

Maita: I am a Christian, the way I teach Paul is on a Christian point of view. Just to take everyone is equal. So if he learns with those things I think he won't fail fitting in well at the society.

As such, there was a relative openness to other worldviews, but largely within the context of moving towards a secular school patron (Educate Together or, arguably, Community National School) paradigm. The possibility that present-day Catholic schools could do more to educate about different religions and ambiguity and doubt across worldviews was rarely raised. Catholic adult participants' data also demonstrated that children's worldviews were framed primarily in terms of a more progressive future rather than examining the present. The discourse of *later* religious choice aligned with neoliberal policy discourses of self-reliance and flexibility. Certainly, participants of various backgrounds were often in favour of diversifying school types, typically by increasing the number of secular patron-run schools, as favoured by the current government. But the problem arising was that there was no significant will to explicitly challenge the patronage system itself, to challenge schools to reflect on ambiguity in their ethos, or to challenge the marketisation of schooling, all of which contribute to the system's inherent majoritarianism. Neither was there a clear motivation regarding engaging wonder, religious uncategorisability, and mystery as public education concerns.

Conclusion

This chapter has demonstrated two key points. First, as we know, adults' orientations towards children and education are shaped by childhood experiences and memories of past experiences. Second, in conjunction with the dynamics of mobility and place discussed in chapter two, such experiences become learned from in a way that aligns with present public and political discourses. Neoliberal policy enactments present the future as premised on individual choice, responsibility and self-reliance. Such imaginings of the future disavow sideways growth – the ways that adults constantly relate to images of a child/childhoods, and the unchosen complexities of their socio-religious experience. Despite differences in interpretations of childhood and education, and new processes of constructing socio-religious culture in urban areas, participants who were raised Catholic tended to have a limited desire to challenge majoritarianism and engage with plurality (in a way that does not seek to commodify it).

Neoliberal policy and public discourses of linear and universal social progress through choice paper over diverse experiences and imaginings of childhoods past, present and future. They disavow the ghosts of institutionalisation present in the pain and exclusion of minority and working-class children and families whose embodied experience is marginalised in favour of majority norms, rhythms and perceptions. In particular, race, class and gender injustices are culturally perpetuated through public criticism of 'failed' (Traveller, working-class) consumption of childhood socio-religious material culture.[21]

The notion that memories of childhood are an important means of engaging ethico-political issues (and specifically engagement with plurality) is not new. Gino and Desai's psychological study[22] contends that priming adults to remember childhood events promotes prosocial behaviour, because such priming heightens adults' perceived sense of children's moral purity, innocence and virtuousness. We did not consciously aim to 'prime' adults to engage with plurality as they recalled the past, and, as chapters one, three and four indicate, it is counterproductive and simplistic to spread imaginaries of childhood as pure and innocent. Nevertheless, I contend through the analysis presented in this chapter that we need to examine how memory works, and exploration of the historic and contemporary material culture of Irish childhoods could support public engagement with difference or plurality, that is, being open to alternative encounters with schools, to the unconscious, and to viewing the familiar – including material culture – in alternative (side)ways.

Returning to Halbwachs, engaging with memory from an ethical perspective reveals that 'the apparent persistence of the same groups merely reflects the external distinctions resulting from places, names, and the general character of societies'. Even our 'most personal remembrances . . . derive from a fusion of diverse and separate elements' in a 'current of continuous thought' and feeling.[23] The increasingly dominant public representation of worldviews as choices is a secularist ethico-political loss. In other words, it is a missed opportunity to engage both with the complex, agentic, sensory and non-instrumental ways children and adults come to embody transcendent and/or worldly orientations. While processes of constructing socio-religious cultures are deeply relational, participants often conflated personal religious autonomy with individual choice, and passively imagined an inclusive school future, instead of thinking about how to create that future in the present. In the context of majority Catholic schooling, the capturing of personal religious autonomy within wider societal processes of individualisation and self-interest also takes attention away from the contribution that collective parish/ community supports can make – despite the very low number of vocations to religious life.

Nevertheless, for majority and broadly advantaged groups such as Catholics, turning to individualism itself involves a form of collective solidarity that excludes others. Deep confrontation with the solidarities and ghosts present in majority collective memory and practice, then, need to be seriously considered as part of public and political discourse that ethically responds to injustices in schooling and childhood in Ireland's present and future. The next chapter will summarise the perspectives, issues and themes examined across the book, with a particular focus on these multiple modes and questions of accountability towards known and unknown others.

6

Building Affirmative, Unchosen School Publics

Introduction

A great deal of courage and creativity is needed to develop forms of representation that do justice to the complexities of the kind of subjects we have already become.[1]

In this chapter, I use the critical postsecular perspective developed throughout the book to draw conclusions about two key aspects of childhood, religion and school injustice in the context of neoliberal education policy enactments and Catholic majoritarianism. The first set of conclusions relates to the issue of school patronage in Ireland and unchosen school publics. The notion of 'unchosen' school publics as discussed here involves, perhaps counterintuitively, committing to particular kinds of anti-majoritarian, postsecular freedoms. The second set of conclusions relates to the everyday curricular experiences of children as they move through school, encounter the world and engage with existential questions about life, death, joy, pain, sacrifice and indulgence.

The plural child/adult is formed through multiple relations to others throughout the life course, and is thus not free to cast aside various attachments in the calculating, self-interested way that neoliberal policies and cultures prioritise. The goal of the chapter is to support education and social movements in building affirmative, unchosen postsecular school publics, which engage us as both individually and collectively plural entities. The purpose of this public engagement is not to compromise or undermine individual and community identities, but to move away from reproduction of fixed, hierarchical dichotomies of individual/society, secular/religious, Christian/atheist to, as Adriana Cavarero asserts, 'begin new things', at least in public education contexts.[2] But first, it must be considered that a great deal of building postsecular school publics requires a rethinking of what we mean by secular freedom and progressiveness.

Dispensing with Progress? Freedoms as Non-linear

Governance of the modern European project has historically involved the persistent citation of a discourse of secular time. Judith Butler identifies secular time as a set of conceptions about history that rely on a view of freedom as something that emerges 'through time, and which is temporally progressive in its structure'.[3] Secular time is a problematic construct, as it imposes an illusion of societal emancipation from various forms of oppressions as if they each had a discrete origin. The construct fails to recognise that religiosities must be included in any claims to secular progressiveness. In the realm of education, Mary Lou Rasmussen urges circumspection about claims to educational freedom, which consign religious investments (and implicitly, non-scientific commitment) to notions of oppression and private interest, and which elevate certain forms of knowledge to the status of unquestionable secular authority.[4] She argues for an affirmative engagement of religious investments within the realm of public (sexuality) education. The goal is not to capitulate to religious (or other) conservatisms, but to complicate them in an engaged public forum. This point sets the tone for the conclusion of this book.

Of course, many emancipatory shifts can be identified in Ireland. In the past five years alone, over a dozen equality-based (Educate Together) second-level schools have been established in the Republic. Same-sex marriage has been legalised in the Republic, and abortion decriminalised across the island. The British government has also passed regulations legalising same-sex marriage in Northern Ireland. But these shifts are themselves complex, and are entangled with a variety of oppressions, not least the suspicion the state levels at LGBT+ asylum seekers. Inhuman developments abound; for example, the Republic's homeless figures are at record-breaking levels. As I wrote the first draft of this final chapter (April 2019), Ireland's Mother and Baby Homes Commission of Investigation released its fifth interim report, as part of a series of investigations into the deaths and burials of thousands of infants and children who died in these homes. In the same week, journalist Lyra McKee was also fatally shot during riots in Derry. In some ways it is difficult to believe that such gendered and heteronormative violence, tied variously to poverty, unemployment and sectarianism, are being inflicted or uncovered two decades into the twenty-first century.

However, dispensing with secular time, when we let go of the illusion that late capitalist societies are on a steady, linear path to uniform freedom – or indeed any reasonable measure of collective freedom – it is not difficult to see why such wounds continue to be inflicted or uncovered. Contemporary violence and scaremongering in Ireland, including the containment and deportation of asylum seekers and systemic racism against Travellers, is part of a global post-colonial context now framed by entrenched post-austerity, racialised neoliberalism and nationalism. The shifts that are actually made through the work of emancipatory social movements are often precarious, because of the particular historic and geographic contexts in which they are situated. Right-wing, nationalist (for example, Brexit, Hindutva) sentiment and neoliberal policy logics of acceptable and unacceptable forms of diversity are key features of the global socio-political landscape. The rapid playing out of these dynamics on media platforms and technologies also adds a surreal, if sometimes useful, level of public scrutiny.

Certain violences have been apologised for by Irish governments and certain religious leaders, with strong statements about 'shameful' parts of Ireland's history. As Nilmini Fernando's work demonstrates, however, the incarceration of maternal bodies in Magdalene Laundries, Mother and Baby Homes and contemporary Direct Provision centres suggests that the temporality of personally experienced, but politically inflicted, shame and pain are reiterated anew by private–public agencies across time and space.[5] In spite, or perhaps because of their conceited liberalism, the sovereign right to kill, to allow to live, or expose to death is a contemporary mode of 'necropolitical' governance that wealthy, global, northern countries are predominantly responsible for. As Achille Mbembe addresses, this is the case not least due to settler colonialism, privatised armies, high-tech wars framed as 'humanitarian' interventions, and associated twenty-four-hour media updates which fail to recognise this entanglement.[6]

Certainly, secular–religious relations in Ireland are changing, with Catholic schools unevenly becoming reconstituted as public spaces. But, as chapter two showed, building on O'Mahony's work, the question of who that varied public is, is complex.[7] The data here also showed that policy encouragement of 'active parent choice' provided racialised, classed and gendered freedoms for the few. The differences between rural and urban contexts can also be stark for different reasons when it comes to attempting to access particular kinds of schools. It is also important not to be complacent about the capacity to be inhuman that neoliberal and nationalist ideologies engender and, as Avery Gordon argues, to 'reckon generously' with ghosts and offer them 'a hospitable memory out of a concern for justice'.[8] From a critical postsecular perspective, we need to engage the non-linear trajectories and persistent necessities of emancipatory social movements, who are typically not given credit for pushing secular freedoms. In 'becoming public', there is no linear march towards a uniformly emancipatory horizon for a school system. This does not mean that calls for education policy and social movements to be emancipatory cannot be mobilised. It also does not mean that we cannot map political steps to change a school landscape. What it does mean is that the unchosen and unknown dimensions of pursuing certain freedoms need to be accepted, and understandings of our freedoms as multiply entangled need to be engaged.

Unchosen School Publics: Pain, Freedom and Becoming Public

Braidotti argues that negative effects of exclusion, pain and violence must be morphed into 'productive and sustainable praxis, which does not deny the reality of horrors, violence and destruction of our times, but propose a different way of dealing with them'.[9] Rather than formulating future understandings of secular freedom in school systems on the basis of one assumed version of the present problem and a fixed model for the future, we must engage multiple, unchosen, socially just relations with known and unknown others. A variety of past, present and future childhoods and schools exist and insist alongside, behind and underneath the current, unjust education policy terrain of enabling active, self-interested choice.

> The conditions for political and ethical agency are not dependent on the current state of the terrain: they are not oppositional and thus not tied to the present by negation. Instead, they are projected across time as affirmative praxis, geared to creating empowering relations aimed at possible futures. Ethical relations create possible worlds by mobilizing resources that have been left untapped in the present, including our desires and imagination . . . Such a vision, moreover, does not restrict the ethical instance within the limits of human otherness, but also opens it up to interrelations with non-human, post-human, and inhuman forces. The eco-philosophical dimension is essential to the postsecular turn in that it values one's reliance on the multiple ecologies that sustain us in a nature–culture continuum (Haraway, 1997; Guattari, 1995, 2000) and within which subjects must cultivate affirmative ethical relations.[10]

204

It is necessary from a critical postsecular perspective to imagine and continue to build movements and spaces that are attuned to education policy and school governance in Ireland becoming public. Becoming public, to again echo Biesta's work, denotes a multi-faceted and somewhat precarious and non-linear process of emancipatory intervention and engagement on education policy discourse and everyday school and child cultures. I use the phrase 'continue to build movements and spaces' in relation to becoming public above, to acknowledge the past and present work of mothers and children in particular, including those participants encountered in this book – in negotiating school types and knowledge about schools and localities. The phrase naturally also includes social movements – including various activists, patrons and politicians – who understand that freedom for oneself is tarnished and narrow, if it does not include meaningful freedoms for marginalised, known and unknown others.

What about (my) freedom?

As discussed in the Introduction and chapter two, the self-interested, privatised and increasingly marketised freedoms offered by education policy tend to present schools and adults' worldviews as fully formed. When worldviews are explored in the space of a dedicated private school, the privatised freedoms expressed may be very meaningful for many. But when placed in public political spheres, these freedoms are deeply limited because they typically give rise to, and maintain, classed, racialised and gendered injustices. Marketised freedom of conscience in education is oriented towards capturing the 'distinctiveness' of a particular secular/religious tradition as a brand. Drawing on Hannah Arendt, Biesta discusses how we can understand freedom in a manner that challenges individual, majoritarian and market self-interest and aligns with the critical postsecular perspective that I have presented in this book.

> Freedom should not be understood as a phenomenon of the will, that is as the freedom to do whatever one chooses to do, but that we should instead conceive of it as the freedom 'to call something into being which did not exist before' (Arendt 1977: 151) . . . freedom is not an 'inner feeling' or a private experience but something that is by necessity a public and hence a political phenomenon.[11]

This understanding of freedom echoes the discussion and analysis of children's ethics in chapter four. Braidotti argues that ethical behaviour 'confirms, facilitates and enhances the subject's *potential* as the capacity to express his or her freedom'.[12] This concept of freedom is fundamentally based on cultivating joy and transforming pain in relation with others, and on the affirmative creations that the unchosen nature of our obligations to known and unknown, human and non-human, others creates.[13] As Saba Mahmood argues similarly in her analysis of the women's piety movement in Egypt, that agency or freedom should not be based in a prescriptive 'binary model of subordination and subversion', as 'the capacity for agency is entailed not only in acts that resist norms but also in the multiple ways one inhabits norms'.[14] As such, we cannot always predict what freedom/agency will look like, but we can be sure that it always involves committing to or being entangled with known and unknown others in specific ways.

Activism for school systems becoming public and cultivating freedom then has both linear and non-linear/unplanned elements and may be focused on 'new arts of existence and ethical relations'.[15] As Braidotti asserts in relation to Foucault's and Deleuze's thought:

> Activism as an affirmative political praxis consists in connecting critical theory not so much to *LA politique* – i.e., organized or majoritarian politics, or "politics as usual" – as to *LE politique* – i.e., the political in its nomadic and transformative forms of becoming . . . Politics (for Deleuze) is postulated on *Chronos* – the linear time of institutional deployment of norms and protocols. It is a reactive and majority-bound enterprise that is often made of flat repetitions and predictable reversals that may alter the balance but leave the structure of power basically untouched. The political, on the other hand, is postulated on the axis of *Aion* – the non-linear time of becoming and of affirmative critical practice. It is minoritarian and it aims at the counter-actualization of alternative states of affairs in relation to the present.[16]

This concept of activism for reform of existing norms and for developing new, perhaps confounding, claims which raise the question of 'how to act' echoes my discussion of acts and practices of anti-racist learner-citizenship elsewhere.[17] There were a number of examples in chapters three and four of how children affirmed, enhanced and expressed their plurality and raised deep ethical questions about the state of current affairs, in predictable and unexpected ways. While easy to ignore as mere play, the children's becomings expressed forms of growing sideways, enhancing their capacity for joy and mitigating suffering in relation to human and non-human, real and symbolic others. Cormac's becoming with comedians and vampires, Lily's becoming with her leopard-print dress, Mia's claim that the church can be funny and holy, Majid's learning from formal Islamic tradition and Spongebob, Grace's critique of learning about religions and her Catholic plurality, Shane's pull into the rhythm of the Fatima Prayer, and Jack's and Ronan's experiences of the transcendent (video gaming, church) all offered glimpses of the potentials to learn and be differently insisting alongside, underneath and beyond their everyday experience.

Their growing sideways with human and non-human others did not create ideal forms of final, complete emancipation. Neither did it suggest that these children were exceptionally heroic, 'resilient' individuals. There were plenty – too many – of examples of ways in which majority children adopted the oppositional, normative consciousness of a politics as usual, and reiterated exclusionary sentiments about devout religious (including older Catholic) and non-religious others. But chapters three and four in particular showed ways that children experience joy or transmute pain into something unique and affirmative, and how they may create songs, myths, stories, maps, movements, questions, looks and images, and use the resources of reason, religion, science and rights to do so. Importantly, the data examined in this book explored children's interactions with each other and the world in a research-based, rather than formal, classroom context. An in-depth focus on curriculum and pedagogy and debates about learning in, from and through religion were beyond the scope of this book. But what the book reveals, as discussed towards the end of this chapter, is the need for understandings of individual children's plurality and engagement with unequal childhoods to form a meaningful part of any public curriculum that teaches about religions, beliefs and ethics. In particular, there is a need to recognise that non-linear growth moves us beyond any notion that children (and, in another given research context, young people) simply reproduce or fail to reproduce particular organised worldviews. The fact of growing sideways itself undermines the absolutisms and rigid worldviews that nationalism thrives upon and that neoliberalism commodifies.

What about adults' part in intergenerational relations?

Certainly, our research did not give adults the same space to wonder, to engage myth and to imagine as it did children. But this is also an artefact of the societal requirement of adults to be rational, fully formed, and to engage with politics on the basis of 'the deployment of norms and protocols . . . that may alter the balance of power but leave the structure of power basically untouched'.[18] This rationalist requirement is an ethico-political problem in and of itself, because, as chapter five demonstrated, affects of fear, wonder, piety and pain that were difficult to put into language, and that saturated past and future childhood imaginaries, were significant to forming adults' worldviews and orientations towards education. Adults exceeded simplistic, self-interested and reductionist notions of present-day school/ worldview choice. They offered glimpses of circular and lateral connections to past and future childhoods through collective, childhood sensory and material culture, family rhythms, transcendent goals, and social obligations. But these connections were often captured by an oversimplified narrative of national progress regarding childhood, which disavowed the inhumanities and inequalities of the past and present and created a false separation between past, present and future pain, joy and obligations. When focused on the individual child's future choices, these imaginaries 'kicked the can down the road', as it were, regarding school and societal change.

It is possible from a public governance perspective to complicate adult-centred notions of religious, spiritual and non-religious sovereign conscience, and to publicly engage wonder, mystery, plurality and opacity within oneself and others, without undermining rights or deep commitments to particular worldviews. This form of public engagement requires reconciling oneself, as Arendt argues, with the 'simultaneous presence of innumerable perspectives . . . for which no common measurement or denominator can ever be devised'.[19] School systems becoming public require, as referenced in chapters one and two, the raising of historical consciousness, growing sideways, acknowledging pain in the present, reimagining collective futures and, ultimately, as Braidotti asserts, enacting 'accountability for the transnational places we all inhabit in late post-modernity'.[20] Exploring the aesthetic and material cultures of childhoods past and future – both with children and adults – appears to me as a key medium through which becoming public can happen at the level of everyday relationships and political activism. There are resources and exemplars developing which can support such exploration at a pedagogical level. Anna Hickey-Moody's transnational Interfaith Childhoods project is a good example of this, one that has the potential to bolster and generate diverse social movements for public education.[21] The Enquiring Classroom project is also noted, towards the end of this chapter, as having significant potential to effect strong, multimodal public engagement with these issues.

However, at a systemic level, as the Forum Advisory Group's 2012 report notes, in the Irish constitution 'the rights of parents for the education of their children is very emphasised, and in

210

(article) 42.3 the State undertakes not to oblige parents to send their children to any school in violation of their conscience'.[22] This constitutional provision assumes that conscience is something fixed, fully formed, known to the parent and relatively unavailable to the child. A clear, chronological, 'politics as usual' element of schools becoming public in the Irish context requires government-supported but social movement-driven re-assessment of the Irish constitution. Developing unchosen school publics in the Irish context requires deep, radical processes of socio-economic and legal reconstruction. This includes examining Ireland's post-colonial obsession with property rights and exploring the compulsory acquisition of schools held by patrons and trustees. These issues were not available to the Forum on Patronage to examine, in the context of policy discourses of 'no alternative' to the massive transfer of international, private losses to people in Ireland. There is, of course, a broader context for examining property rights in Ireland: vulture funds, escalating rents, failure to build public housing, lack of meaningful regulation of private landlords and the resulting accommodation and homeless crisis. Any proposals regarding schools 'opting out' of, for example, the forthcoming public/state Education about Religions and Beliefs (ERB) and Ethics curriculum can only be reasonable if situated in a radical development in public school provision.

Given the failure of patronage divestment to produce deep change, and the resistance to change on the part of those already advantaged, it seems unlikely in Ireland that things will fundamentally change without strong, intergenerational organising that is built on the case for affirmative, unchosen school publics and the necessity of encountering unknown and known others as a positional good. The concept of 'unknown' others refers here not just to those we do not have a direct interpersonal relationship with – nor does it refer to gaining cultural and social capital by commodifying 'diversity'. It refers to the fluidity and final unknowability of our own and others' plurality, as outlined in the next section. Engagement in such formal activist work, while involving to some extent 'politics as usual', also involves the synchronisation of multiple activist affinities and trajectories. This synchronisation cannot make public icons or absolutist figures of the child, nation, science, rights, religion or reason. Rather, emerging from the failure of absolutes and universal common ground, it needs to present alternative societal imaginaries for schools becoming public that problematise neat secular/religious binaries in the present and engage multiple epistemologies/knowledge bases.

The Plural Child and the Public Curriculum

Braidotti's words cited earlier in this chapter regarding the postsecular condition indicate several different issues that merit public, curricular attention. These include everything from the possibilities and limits of post-human technological and scientific amendments to the body, to the severe, existential threat posed by human efforts to control non-human ecologies, to supra-human commitments, for example, to the divine. Rhetorically at least, all of the above topics are entirely within the curricular scope of every primary school in Ireland. They are visible in, and can be considered within, the remit of all state curricular statements (aims, objectives, strands) and supporting guidance: Social, Environmental and Scientific Education (SESE), Civic, Social and Political Education (CSPE), Social,

Personal and Health Education (SPHE), and the proposed Education about Religions and Beliefs and Ethics (ERBE). They are also very much within the scope of patron primary materials and statements, including Follow Me (Church of Ireland, Methodist, Presbyterian and Society of Friends schools), Grow in Love (Catholic schools), Learn Together (Educate Together schools), and Goodness Me Goodness You (Community National schools).

This book does not formally examine curriculum or pedagogy of civil religious education, ethics education or faith formation in secular/religious schools. There are several analyses of the kinds of secular and religious curricula available in Ireland. However, the book does put forward a concept of the plural child and the connected notion of growing sideways,[23] which jars somewhat with the way childhood is explicitly framed and envisaged in current curricular statements and proposals. Given that my focus is on school systems becoming *public*, I will primarily discuss the national curriculum as opposed to patron curricula here. However, it is worth noting that the child's plurality insists underneath, between and all around the methodologies recommended in these curricula/their associated guidelines. The patron curricula named above present the epistemology (or the knowledge base) of the curriculum in an interdisciplinary way. For example, the most recently released patron curriculum statement Goodness Me Goodness You (for third to sixth class, or nine to twelve years) states that 'across the curriculum, a pluralist epistemology and pedagogy is put into action which seeks to develop different aspects of children's potential'.[24] All of the patron curricula named above engage the importance of narrative and wider arts which, as chapters three and four indicate, are so crucial to children's encounters with the world.

They also all, to varying degrees, educate children in, or are aligned with, reason, science and rights-based thinking and approaches to the world.

It is also worth noting that specific faith formation is not a prescribed feature of Church of Ireland schools, not least due to their Christian interdenominational focus. Given the historic association of Catholic schools with 'the public to be educated', and the clearly varied nature of that public (now and in the past), my view is that it is not tenable for sacramental preparation to continue during the school day in Catholic primary schools. However, focusing on this issue misses the earlier point about the broader 'becoming public' of schools, and about property rights at constitutional and legislative levels. The same point can be made about the state Education about Religions and Beliefs (ERB) and Ethics curriculum. This curriculum is in the process of formation, on foot of recommendations from the Advisory Group to the Forum on Patronage and Pluralism. The ERB and Ethics discussion document outlines four possible approaches: that it would be part of the existing patron (religious or secular education) programme; that it would be integrated across curricular areas; that it would be a discrete curriculum; or that it would have discrete and integrated components.[25] At the time of writing, the principles of the proposed curriculum are:

1. ERB and Ethics should enable children to develop self-awareness, confidence, personal beliefs and positive social identities.
2. ERB and Ethics should enable children to have a knowledge and understanding of how religions and belief traditions have contributed to the culture in which we live.

3. ERB and Ethics should enable children to express comfort, empathy and joy with human diversity.
4. ERB and Ethics should enable children to form deep, caring human connections.
5. ERB and Ethics should enable children to understand the relationship between rights and responsibilities.
6. ERB and Ethics should enable children to appreciate the impact of prejudice and discrimination.[26]

A degree of opposition to the above principles is evident in the publicly available written submissions to the NCCA, which is not surprising. However the above aims have been welcomed in survey research by varying majorities of educators and parents engaged through the formal consultation process.[27] The strands of personal understanding, mutual understanding, spiritual awareness, character education and connection to the wider world were also welcomed by majorities. Interestingly, parents participating in the survey regarding these stated aims were more supportive of 'aims and ideas relating to social justice and personal development' than aspects such as 'curiosity about religions' and 'contribution of religions'.[28] It was also interesting that, amongst educators, the notion that a particular theme was 'already covered by the current curriculum emerged as a response across different questions'.[29] The benign view might be that this response indicates legitimate educator concerns about curricular overload (which was articulated as a challenge, separately, in educator responses). A more cynical view might be that this response papers over these publicly oriented proposals with bad-faith notions of 'interdisciplinarity' and patron curricula 'already doing' such work.

It is in some ways facile to critique a consultation document on the proposed Education about Religion and Beliefs (ERB) and Ethics curriculum – the curriculum itself is a welcome proposal. There is a wider point to be made, however, that the proposed curriculum, and other national curriculum statements and guidelines, do not take the explicit step of inviting schools to carefully and respectfully explore religious/non-religious, individual/community, individual/society and culture/nature binaries that are used to define, categorise and individualise the plural self. The data in chapters three and four indicate there is great potential for such careful exploration. From a critical postsecular perspective, such exploration would need to have a stated purpose of enriching, rather than undermining, understandings of the religious and ethical commitments of children and families, and protecting against the presentation or institutionalisation of one monolithic worldview as superior to others in the classroom, school and wider societal contexts.

Unfortunately, none of the above guidelines explicitly makes any room for a concept of the person as plural, as growing in creative ways that are not linked to linear notions of development, in relation to human and non-human others beyond these binaries. This is not surprising, as the meaning of difference/plurality is typically assumed rather than clearly defined in contemporary European curricular statements and guidelines. Sharon Todd argues that the key means put forward for engaging the 'problem' of difference in European intercultural documents is *dialogue*, which, she argues, essentialises differences as fixed individual or group traits that people speak 'from'.[30] Todd substitutes a radical conception of plurality for this concept of diversity, to attend to the unique, particular, changing persons/coalitions that emerge in ongoing encounters, and to avoid repeatedly reducing personhood to representational logics and immutable (socially stratified) identities. In Todd's view, the polis is a relational, narrative space that is unpredictable in its telling. The person's uniqueness does not appear through individualised development but 'in the in-between space with other human beings' through narratives told in interaction with others.[31] Here, the focus is not on substance (for example, a fixed meaning for a sign or symbol, identity categories, or body):

> Rather the political essence of speech consists in revealing to others the uniqueness of each speaker . . . whereupon those present show to one another, in their words and deeds, their uniqueness and their capacity to begin new things ([Cavarero 2005, p. 89] in Todd 2011, p. 107).[32]

It is understandable, and helpful, given the Catholic majoritarian nature of the school system, that the ERBE consultation document aligns itself with the Toledo Principles for teaching about religions and beliefs in a way that is 'sufficiently objective'.[33] In other words, 'objectivity' is not considered an absolute value. It is encouraging that affects of comfort and joy are considered important to explicitly mention as part of the proposed aims of the curriculum (even if these are only linked, as above, to 'human diversity' and 'human connections'). The discussion document's refusal to make an icon out of rationalism is positive, and aligns with the notion of a 'residual spirituality' that Braidotti reserves for critical thought.[34] Several elements of the discussion document incorporate other principles of deep engagement with plurality, as outlined in chapter one, and, naturally, sustainable development and environmental concerns are given a central role. It is worrying, however, given the scale of ecological crisis that faces all life, that, in the discussion document and pre-existing primary curriculum documents, humanity's radical enmeshing with non-human entities, including animals, plants, and digital technologies, is positioned as secondary to 'the precious nature of human existence'. It is difficult to see how children and schools are to 'begin new things' across Irish and European education contexts when there is a failure to meaningfully conceptualise the human as *intra*-acting with, as opposed to interacting with or acting on, human and non-human others. Notwithstanding the potential for integration across disciplines in schools, the principles behind the discussion document also miss the opportunity to present an embodied, geographic and historic understanding of ethics: to understand how ethical relations are built, based on specific locations in time and space that, as discussed in chapter one, encourage us to:

> Embrace certain things in this particular place, to be indifferent to some, to be wary of others, and to fight militantly against the continuation of yet others . . . pluralists set limits to tolerance to ensure that an exclusionary . . . movement does not take over an entire regime.[35]

Certainly, the curricular principles above focus on enabling children to 'appreciate the impact of prejudice and discrimination', but 'appreciating' is no substitute for *challenging* multiple axes of prejudice and discrimination in specific places. In this regard, there is a deep need for 'creative links and zigzagging interconnections between discursive communities that are too often kept apart from each other'.[36]

Finally, there is no exploration of the entanglements of advanced consumer capitalism and material culture with socio-religious tradition, which is a core feature of children's experiences, as explored in this book. Children's entanglements with non-human material culture tend to fall into moralising traps, particularly regarding consumption. Certainly, this book critiques consumerist and other types of self-interest. But not all consumption practices are equally problematic, as they exist in classed, racialised and gendered systems of value. Indeed, the forms of consumption that marginalised religious (adult, child) bodies perform can help make those bodies sites of relative resistance to classed and racialised stigma.[37] The messy material culture of traditionally religious and mass consumer objects that we are variously part of must be treated sensitively, as part of our ethical accountability to each other.[38]

Of course, curricular statements and books are not a reflection of the enacted and experienced curriculum explored by the practice network associated with the ERB and Ethics consultations. Indeed, ethical and philosophical explorations provided for in these curricula may yield many new beginnings. However, the discussion document does set certain precedents, and the curriculum review/formulation process itself reflects the acceptability and reproducibility of certain forms of curricular vision. A positive development linked into the ERB and Ethics curriculum, as noted on the NCCA website, is the Enquiring Classroom project.[39] This project, led by Aislinn O'Donnell and Patricia Kieran in Ireland, and developed with other European partners, is targeted at a spectrum of children, young people and adults. It presents pedagogical principles and resources that offer some possibilities for deep engagement with plurality. The way that the project is framed, around 'Rough Guide to the Sacred (the religious and the secular)', 'Living Values (the ethical)', 'Thinking Together (the philosophical)', 'Encountering the World (the aesthetic)', 'Engaging with Tradition (the past and the historical)' and 'Difficult Conversations (moments of stuckness and perplexity)' is creative. The pedagogies are embodied and involve movement, sitting, gathering, sound, silence, drawing, writing, storytelling, amongst others. More room needs to be made in this kind of work for systemic and decolonial thinking which acknowledges the historical context that such interactions emerge from. But such creative, arts-oriented/aesthetically sensitised approaches create great scope for both rational and spiritual engagement. They also facilitate 'refrains'. As discussed in the Introduction to this book, Maggie MacLure uses the concept of 'refrains' to refer to moments where words, phrases and images are detached from the order in which they normally appear and are experimented with. Refrains emerge 'via contagion, affect, and epidemic rather than by meaning' and interrupt the prevailing way of thinking and feeling about things.[40] They have the contagious potential to open up new trajectories of ethical desire, imagination and accountability. It is time, then, to sensitise our educational encounters not just to pre-existing rationalities and affects, but to refrains, to the new, to the already-existing and insisting inside, alongside and underneath what we take for granted as the everyday.

Conclusion

We know that Catholic majoritarianism is not *the* (only) problem in the school sector in Ireland or indeed elsewhere. Any engagement of childhood, religion and school injustice cannot turn away from multiple related problems created by neoliberal and nationalist education policy enactments. I have argued in this chapter that we need to place childhood, religion and school injustice in the above, broader socio-political context of the multiple, precarious forms of freedom, new and old forms of symbolic and physical violence, unexpected turns and, of course, the severe ecological precariousness that characterises the postsecular condition. In Ireland, this requires continuing to build education and social movements that challenge white, settled, Catholic Irish majoritarianism, and the colonial, classed, racialised and gendered patronage model that underpins it. It requires public policy interventions, which do away with the neoliberal fantasy and colonial legacy of an equally choosing consumer–citizenry. It requires creative engagements with public education in a way that builds and explores affirmative relationships between past, present and future imaginaries of childhood and schooling, and the material cultures of consumption and faith. Deep engagement with plurality does not require the ending of religious/faith or private schooling, but it does require the substantial building of school publics and experiences based affirmatively on our unchosen obligations to known and unknown others. The task entails not presuming or fixing in advance who we or others can be in terms of our worldviews or experiences. It requires, as Braidotti states, engaging resources 'left untapped in the present . . . including our desire and imagination'.

Endnotes

Introduction. Childhood, Religion and School Injustice

1   A. Mawhinney, *Freedom of Religion and Schools* (Saarbrücken: VDM Verlag, 2009); E. Daly, *Religion, Law and the Irish State* (Dublin: Clarus Press, 2012); C. O'Mahony, *Educational Rights in Irish Law* (Dublin: Thomson Round Hall, 2006).

2   G. Byrne and P. Kieran (eds), *Toward Mutual Ground* (Dublin: The Columba Press, 2013); M. Shanahan (ed.), *Does Religious Education Matter?* (London: Routledge, 2017).

3   D. Devine, *Immigration and Schooling in the Republic of Ireland* (Manchester: Manchester University Press, 2011); K. Fischer, *Schools and the Politics of Religion and Diversity in the Republic of Ireland* (Manchester: Manchester University Press, 2016).

4   J. Deegan, D. Devine and A. Lodge (eds), *Primary Voices* (Dublin: Institute of Public Adminstration, 2004); J. Berglund, Y. Shanneik and B. Bocking (eds), *Religious Education in a Global-Local World* (Cham, Switzerland: Springer, 2016); E. Smyth, M. Lyons and M. Darmody (eds), *Religious Education in a Multicultural Europe* (Basingstoke: Palgrave 2013).

5   E. O'Mahony, *Religious and Secular Places* (PhD thesis, National University of Ireland Maynooth, 2015).

6   A. Neary, *LGBT-Q Teachers, Civil Partnership and Same-Sex Marriage* (London: Routledge, 2017).

7   K. Crenshaw, 'Mapping the Margins: Intersectionality, Identity Politics and Violence against Women of Color', *Stanford Law Review*, vol. 43, 1991, pp. 1241–1299.

8   R. Braidotti, *Nomadic Theory: The Portable Rosi Braidotti* (New York: Columbia University Press, 2011), p. 171.

9   G. Bhattacharyya, 'Racial Neoliberal Britain?', in N. Kapoor, V.S. Kalra and J. Rhodes (eds), *The State of Race* (Basingstoke: Palgrave Macmillan, 2013), pp. 31–48; E. Rowe, C. Lubienski, A. Skourdoumbis, J. Gerrard and D. Hursh, 'Templates, Typologies and Typifications: Neoliberalism as Keyword', *Discourse*, vol. 40, 2019, pp. 150–161.

10 A. Lentin and G. Titley, *The Crises of Multiculturalism: Racism in a Neoliberal Age* (London: Zed Books, 2011).

11 S. Bruce, 'Religion and Rational Choice', *Sociology of Religion*, vol. 54, 1993, pp. 193–205.

12 G. Meaney, 'Race, Sex and Nation', *The Irish Review*, vol. 35, 2007, pp. 51–52.

13 N. Chandhoke, *Rethinking Pluralism, Secularism and Tolerance: Anxieties of Coexistence* (London: Sage, 2019).

14 Pew Research Centre, *Being Christian in Western Europe* (Pew Research Centre, 2018).

15 J.A. Beckford, *Cult Controversies* (London: Tavistock, 1985). This stigmatising public focus has appeared more systematically in recent years for at least two reasons. The first is the heightened significance of bodily image, size, shape, symbols and technologies to globalised, neoliberal governing projects. The second is, as Beckford argues, that religious expression can become more sensationalised as it becomes less salient in a given society.

16 H. Bacon, W. Dossett and S. Knowles (eds), *Alternative Salvations* (New York: Bloomsbury, 2015); E. Burman, 'Brexit, "Child as Method," and the Pedagogy of Failure', *Review of Education, Pedagogy and Culture*, vol. 40, 2018, pp. 119–143. Ironically, this secular narrative is often steeped in colonial, conservative religious salvation/rescue tropes, which ignore the structural injustices surrounding children, their families and adult–child intergenerational relationships, states and feelings.

17 R. Braidotti, 'Feminist Epistemology After Postmodernism', *Interdisciplinary Science Reviews*, vol. 32, 2007, p. 66.

18 G. Biesta, 'Becoming Public', *Social and Cultural Geography*, vol. 13, 2012, p. 683.

19 M. Nye, *Religion* (London: Routledge, 2008), p. 3.

20 B. de Sousa Santos, '*Nuestra America*: Reinventing a Subaltern Paradigm of Recognition and Redistribution', *Theory, Culture and Society*, vol. 18, 185–217; G.C. Spivak, 'Can the Subaltern Speak?', in P. Williams and L. Chrisman (eds), *Colonial Discourse and Post-Colonial Theory: A Reader* (London: Harvester, 1993), pp. 66–112.

21 B. Davies, *Listening to Children: Being and Becoming* (London: Routledge, 2014).

22 A.F. Gordon, *Ghostly Matters* (Minneapolis: University of Minnesota Press, 2008).

23 Braidotti, 'Feminist Epistemology', p. 67.

24 G. Hage, *Alter-Politics* (Melbourne: Melbourne University Press, 2015); R. Braidotti, 'Residual Spirituality'.

25 J. Beckford, 'Public Religions and the Postsecular', *Journal for the Scientific Study of Religions*, vol. 51, 2012, pp. 1–19.

26 R. Braidotti, B. Blaagaard, T. de Graauw and E. Midden, 'Introductory Notes', in R. Braidotti, B. Blaagaard, T. de Graauw and E. Midden (eds), *Transformations of Religion and the Public Sphere* (Basingstoke: Palgrave Macmillan, 2014), pp. 1–13.

27 G.K. Bhambra, *Rethinking Modernity* (Basingstoke: Palgrave, 2007); *Connected Sociologies* (London: Bloomsbury, 2014).

28 Braidotti et al, 'Introductory Notes', p. 2.

29 Braidotti et al, 'Introductory Notes', p. 4.

30 R. Braidotti, 'The Residual Spirituality in Critical Theory', in R. Braidotti, B. Blaagaard, T. de Graauw, and E. Midden (eds), *Transformations of Religion and the Public Sphere* (Basingstoke: Palgrave Macmillan, 2014), pp. 249–272.

31 Department of Education and Skills, *Key Statistics 2016/2017 and 2017/2018* (Dublin: Government Stationery Office, 2018).

32 K. Kitching, 'A Thousand Tiny Pluralities', *Critical Studies in Education*, online.

33 E. O'Kelly, 'Parents Need to Make Informed Choices over School Patronage' (RTÉ News, 3 April 2019; E. O'Kelly, 'Third Dublin School Sends Letter Warning of Consequences over Changing Patronage' (RTÉ News, 3 April 2019). Based on a survey of local preschool parents in North Dublin, the Archbishop of Dublin, Diarmuid Martin, began a process of exploring the divestment of one Catholic school in the area to a multidenominational patron. Letters were sent from two of the Catholic schools to parents. These letters variously claimed multidenominational schools would not celebrate Christmas, or St Patrick's Day, or indeed, Halloween, or that it may no longer be possible to celebrate the role of grandparents in children's lives.

34 Berglund et al., *Religious Education in a Global-Local World*.

35 V. Malsevic, 'Ireland and Neo-Secularisation Theory', *Irish Journal of Sociology*, vol. 18, pp. 22–42.

36 Devine, *Immigration and Schooling*; Byrne and Kieran, *Toward Mutual Ground*.

37 R.A. Davis, 'Religion, Education and the Post-secular Child', *Critical Studies in Education*, vol. 55, 2014, p. 20. Davis acknowledges that Childhood Studies has created an 'infinitely richer and globalised comparative anthropology of childhood', which is 'directly descended from the breakthroughs of feminism'.

38 See, for example, B. Davies, *Listening to Children* (London: Routledge, 2015); M.L. Rasmussen, *'Progressive' Sexuality Education* (London:

Routledge 2015); A.C. Hickey-Moody, 'Arts Practice as Method, Urban Spaces and Intra-active Faiths', *International Journal of Inclusive Education*, vol. 21, 2017, pp. 1083–1096; E. Renold, J. Ringrose and R.D. Egan (eds), *Children, Sexuality and Sexualization* (Hampshire: Palgrave Macmillan, 2015).

39 Davies, *Listening*, p. 35.

40 B. de S. Santos, 'If God Were a Human Rights Activist: Human Rights and the Challenge of Political Theologies', *Law, Social Justice and Global Development Journal*, vol. 1, http://go.warwick.ac.uk/elj/lgd/2009_1/santos.

41 S. Mahmood, 'Religious Reason and Secular Affect', *Critical Inquiry*, vol. 35, 2009, pp. 842–843. Mahmood argues it is commonly assumed that devout persons can choose to distinguish between a worldly object (e.g. the cross) and divine or venerated subjects (e.g. Allah or the Prophet Mohammed, respectively). Such assumptions fail to account not only for Islamic, but also certain Christian and ancient Greek traditions.

42 P.M. Cooey, 'Neither Seen nor Heard: The Absent Child in the Study of Religion', *Journal of Childhood and Religion*, vol. 1, 2010, pp. 1–31.

43 Cooey, 'Neither Seen nor Heard p. 12.

44 Mahmood, 'Religious Reason', pp. 848–849. Mahmood argues further that the injury regarding the cartoon emanates 'not from the judgment that the law has been transgressed but that one's being, grounded as it is in a relationship of dependency with the Prophet, has been shaken'.

45 Hickey-Moody, 'Arts Practice', p. 1091.

46 Davies, *Listening to Children*; H. Lenz Taguchi, *Going Beyond the Theory/Practice Divide in Early Childhood Education: Introducing an Intra-Active Pedagogy* (London: Routledge/Falmer, 2010); G. Dahlberg and P. Moss, *Ethics and Politics in Early Childhood Education* (London: Routledge/Falmer, 2005).

47 M. MacLure, 'The Refrain of the A-Grammatical Child', *Cultural Studies – Critical Methodologies*, vol. 16, 2016, p. 179.

48 J. Butler, *Giving an Account of Oneself* (New York: Fordham University Press, 2005).

49 K. Bond Stockton, *The Queer Child, or Growing Sideways in the Twentieth Century* (Durham: Duke University Press, 2009).

50 W.E. Connolly, *Pluralism* (Durham: Duke University Press, 2005).

51 J. Coolahan, C. Hussey and P. Kilfeather, *The Forum on Patronage and Pluralism* (Dublin: Department of Education and Skills, 2012).

52 W. Weisse, 'RedCo: A European Research Project on Religion in Education', *Religion and Education*, vol. 37, 2010, pp. 187–202.

53 A. Amin, 'Ethnicity and the Multicultural City: Living with Diversity', *Environment and Planning A*, vol. 34, 2002, p. 970.

54 Amin, 'Ethnicity and the Multicultural City'.

55 Amin, 'Ethnicity and the Multicultural City', p. 969.

56 J. Irwin, 'Existential Thought between Ethics and Religion as Related to Curriculum: From Kierkegaard to Sartre', in M. Shanahan (ed.), *Does Religious Education Matter?* (London: Routledge, 2017).

57 O'Mahony, *Religious and Secular Places*, p. 60.

58 Irish Episcopal Conference, *Catholic Preschool and Primary Religious Education Curriculum for Ireland* (Dublin: Veritas, 2015).

59 M. Heinz, K. Davison and E. Keane, 'I Will Do It But Religion is a Very Personal Thing', *European Journal of Teacher Education*, vol. 41, 2018, pp. 232–245.

60 O'Mahony, *Religious and Secular Places*, p. 145.

61 R. Byrne and D. Devine, 'Catholic Schooling with a Twist? A Study of Faith Schooling in the Republic of Ireland during a Period of Detraditionalisation', *Cambridge Journal of Education*, vol. 48, 2018, pp. 461–477.

62 N. Yuval-Davis, 'Power, Intersectionality and the Politics of Belonging' (FREIA Working Paper Series, 2011), http://vbn.aau.dk/files/58024503/FREIA_wp_75.pdf.

63 N. Fraser, 'Rethinking the Public Sphere', *Social Text*, vol. 25/26, 1990, pp. 56–80.

64 J. Qvortrup, 'Varieties of Childhood', in J. Qvortrup (ed.), *Studies in Modern Childhood* (Hampshire: Palgrave Macmillan, 2005), pp. 1–20.

65 A. Hickey Moody, 'Little Public Spheres', *Performance Paradigm*, vol. 9, 2013, p. 1.

66 Bhabha, 'Unpacking My Library Again', *The Journal of the Midwest Modern Language Association*, vol. 28, 1995, pp. 5–18.

67 L. Kong, 'Mapping "New" Geographies of Religion', *Progress in Human Geography*, vol. 25, 2001, p. 212.

68 Butler, *Giving an Account of Oneself.*

69 Biesta, 'Becoming Public', p. 683.

70 Braidotti, 'Residual Spirituality', p. 258.

71 H. Alexander, *Reimagining Liberal Education* (London: Bloomsbury, 2015).

72 Braidotti et al., 'Introductory Notes', p. 4.

1. Understanding Worldviews and Placing 'Irish' Childhoods and Schools

1 W.E. Connolly, *Pluralism* (Dublin: Duke University Press, 2005).

2 G.D. Chryssides and M.Z. Wilkins, *A Reader in New Religious Movements* (London: Continuum, 2006).

3 T.A. Tweed, *Crossing and Dwelling*, p. 73. The term 'supra-human' refers to forces broader than God, gods and spiritual beings to include,

for example, the appeal to buddhas in aiding devotional life and non-personified forces such as the Daoist *dao* (way). Tweed notes that the embedding of the supra-human in the human is imagined in some Christian doctrines through the interpretation of humans as created in the image of God, for example, having a symbolic relationship with God, and/or sharing certain characteristics. However, this concept is also interpreted in Islamic doctrines, for example in terms of God having a personal relationship with each individual.

4 T. Asad, *Genealogies of Religion* (Baltimore, MA: John Hopkins University Press, 1993).

5 Mahmood, 'Religious Reason'.

6 Ridgely Bales, *When I Was a Child*.

7 Connolly, *Pluralism*, p. 58; T. Asad, *Formations of the Secular* (Stanford: Stanford University Press, 2003).

8 C. McDannell, *Material Christianity, Religion and Popular Culture in America* (London: Yale University Press, 1995), p. 8.

9 J. Carr, *Experiences of Islamophobia* (London: Routledge, 2016).

10 O'Mahony, *Religious and Secular Places*.

11 Meaney, 'Race, Sex and Nation', *The Irish Review*, vol. 35, 2007, pp. 51–52.

12 J.C. van der Kooij, D.J. de Ruyter and S. Miedema, '"Worldview"', *Religious Education,* vol. 108, 2013, p. 212.

13 D. Houtman and S. Aupers, 'The Spiritual Turn and the Decline of Tradition', *Journal for the Scientific Study of Religion*, vol. 46, 2007, pp. 305–320. Our understanding of what counts and does not count as religion becomes further complicated when we consider the rise of 'New Age' movements and individual practices in recent decades. Many of these movements self-define as spiritual, but not religious in terms of organised religion. Such spirituality (or spiritualities) may be more broadly defined than religiosity (or religiosities), in that it may seek a higher good either in the present world, or in a reality greater than human reality. Transcendence may be sought and expressed through individual or collective activities, including formal religious observance, yoga, martial arts, virtual reality/video gaming or ecological conservation. Houtman and Alpers claim that with the emergence of New Age spiritualities, the sacred loses its transcendent (that is, supernatural or holy) character and becomes relocated to 'deeper layers of the self'. The authenticity of some New Age spiritualities can become questioned because of their involvement in consumerism and individualism. However, as we will see, religious interests are deeply entangled with the history of capitalist, and consumerist societies. The vexed question of authenticity is returned to again and again throughout this book.

227

14 A.G. Nixon, *New Atheism* (Doctoral thesis, University of Western Sydney, 2014).

15 Heinz, Davison and Keane, 'I Will Do it'; K. Kitching and Y. Shanneik, *Children's Beliefs and Belonging* (Cork: Authors, 2015); Smyth et al., *Religious Education*; Burglund et al., *Religious Education*.

16 Burman, *Developments*.

17 Kitching, *The Politics of Compulsive Education*.

18 K. Smith, 'Producing Governable Subjects', *Childhood*, vol. 19, 2001, pp. 24–37.

19 V. Zelizer, *Pricing the Priceless Child* (Princeton: Princeton University Press, 1985). Sacralisation in this sense may refer to the elevation of children's worldly development as a greater good, often expressed contemporarily through the language of individual children's wellbeing and/or rights.

20 D. Devine, '"Value"ing Migrant Children Differently?' *Children and Society*, vol. 27, 2013, pp. 282–294.

21 R. van Krieken, 'The "Best Interests of the Child" and Parental Separation', *The Modern Law Review*, vol. 68, 2005, pp. 25–48.

22 Qvortrup, 'Varieties of Childhood'.

23 S. Henry, 'Education, Queer Theology, and Spiritual Development', *International Journal of Children's Spirituality*, vol. 23, 2018, p. 5.

24 L. Fendler, 'Educating Flexible Souls', in K. Hultqvist and G. Dahlberg (eds), *Governing the Child in the New Millennium* (London: Routledge Falmer, 2001), pp. 119–142.

25 Bond Stockton, *The Queer Child*, pp. 5–6, my brackets. Here, Bond Stockton is specifically referring to the paradoxes of child sexuality. While on the one hand, children are expected to be asexual, they are also typically expected to be on the road to becoming heterosexual.

26 O. Jones, 'Endlessly Revisited and Forever Gone', *Children's Geographies*, vol. 1, 2003, pp. 25–36.

27 Bond Stockton, *The Queer Child*, p. 13.

28 Bond Stockton, *The Queer Child*, p. 15.

29 A.C. Hickey-Moody, 'Deleuze's Children', *Educational Philosophy and Theory*, vol. 45, 2013, pp. 272–286.

30 R. Braidotti, *Transpositions: On Nomadic Theory* (Cambridge: Polity, 2006); Braidotti, 'Residual Spirituality'.

31 Gordon, *Ghostly Matters*, pp. 63–64.

32 Braidotti, *Transpositions*, p. 17.

33 J. Pierce, D.G. Martin and J.T. Murphy, 'Relational Place-Making', *Transactions of the Institute of British Geographers,* vol. 36, 2011, pp. 54–70.

34 Fischer, *Schools*; P. Hemming, 'Educating for Religious Citizenship', *Transactions of the Institute of British Geographers*, vol. 36, 2011, pp. 441–454; L. Kong, 'Religious Schools', *Environment and Planning D*, vol. 23, 2005, pp. 615–631.

35 O'Mahony, *Religious and Secular Places*.

36 O'Mahony, *Religious and Secular Places*, p. 14.

37 E. Larkin, 'The Devotional Revolution in Ireland, 1850–75', *American Historical Review*, vol. 77, pp. 625–652; T. McGrath, 'The Tridentine Evolution of Modern Irish Catholicism', in R. Ó Muirí (ed.), *Irish Church History Today* (Armagh: Cumann Seanchais Ard Mhacha, 1991), pp. 84–99; K. O'Driscoll, *Reform, Instruction and Practice* (PhD thesis, NUI Galway, 2016). As O'Driscoll relates, Larkin's 'devotional revolution theory' suggests a dramatic change in religious practice in almost a generation led by Cardinal Paul Cullen in the second half of the nineteenth century. McGrath's 'Tridentine revolution' argument suggests those practices considered 'new' to Ireland were in fact pre-existing practices approved since the mid-sixteenth-century Council of Trent.

38 T. Inglis, *Moral Monopoly: The Rise and Fall of the Catholic Church in Modern Ireland* (Dublin: University College Dublin Press, 1998).

39 C. Delay, 'Holy Water and a Twig', *Journal of Family History*, vol. 43, 2018, pp. 302–319.

40 Inglis, *Moral Monopoly*, p. 191.

41 M.J. Maguire, *Precarious Childhood in Post-independence Ireland* (Manchester: Manchester University Press, 2009), p. 7.

42 P. McGrail, *First Communion: Ritual, Church and Popular Religious Identity* (Aldershot: Ashgate, 2007), p. 13.

43 B. Fanning, ' A Catholic Vision of Ireland', in T. Inglis (ed.), *Are the Irish Different?* (Manchester: Manchester University Press, 2014), pp. 44–53.

44 O'Mahony, *Religious and Secular Places*.

45 O'Mahony, *Religious and Secular Places*; Lodge, 'First Communion in Carnduffy', *Irish Educational Studies*, vol. 18, pp. 210–222; McGrail, *First Communion*, p. 169

46 T. Inglis, 'Catholic Identity in Contemporary Ireland', *Journal of Contemporary Religion*, vol. 22, 2007, pp. 217–218.

47 Pew Research Center, *Being Christian*.

48 Equate Ireland, *Religion and School: Parents' Voices* (Dublin: Equate Ireland, 2017).

49 Coolahan et al., *The Forum on Patronage and Pluralism*.

50 Catholic Schools Partnership, *Catholic Primary Schools in a Changing Ireland* (Maynooth: Catholic Schools Partnership, 2015).

51 M. Darmody, E. Smyth and S. McCoy, *School Sector Variation Among Primary Schools in Ireland* (Dublin: ESRI and Educate Together, 2012).

The term 'multi-denominational' in the *School Sector Variation* report refers largely to Educate Together schools, a minority of Gaelscoileanna (Irish language schools) run by An Foras Pátrúnachta, and a small number 'managed by Vocational Education Committees' (p. iii). It did not include the then five, now twelve, Community National Schools now run by local (public) Education and Training Boards.

52 Darmody et al., *School Sector Variation*, p. 35.

53 E.F. Isin and G.M. Nielsen, 'Introduction', in E.F. Isin and G.M. Nielsen (eds), *Acts of Citizenship* (London: Zed Books, 2008), pp. 1–12. Citizenship is ordinarily understood as one's political, social and legal rights and obligations pertaining to the nation-state. However, as Isin and Nielsen state, 'environments, markets and sexes are not things for which you can hold legal membership' and 'one can be an environmental, sexual, cosmopolitan and consumer citizen all at once' (p. 1).

54 Hemming, 'Educating for Religious Citizenship'. For Hemming, religious citizenship refers to 'the role of religion in devising criteria for access to state or community membership, the political rights and responsibilities attributed to particular religious groups within that membership' and 'the religious aspects of collective . . . identity that influence belonging' (p. xxx).

55 Smith, 'Producing Governable Subjects', p. 30.

56 Devine, *Immigration and Schooling*; D. Faas, A. Smith and M. Darmody, 'Children's Agency in Multi-Belief Settings', *Journal of Research in Childhood Education*, vol. 32, 2018, pp. 486–500; Kitching and Shanneik, *Children's Beliefs*.

57 Connolly, *Pluralism*, p. 4.

58 Ibid., p. 123.

59 A. Finlayson, 'Introduction: Becoming Plural', in A. Finlayson (ed.), Democracy and Pluralism (London: Routledge, 2010), pp. 3–4.

60 L. Pellandini-Simányi, 'Bourdieu, Ethics and Symbolic Power', *The Sociological Review*, vol. 62, 2014, pp. 651–674.

61 J. Butler, *Undoing Gender* (London: Routledge, 2004).

62 Connolly, *Pluralism*, p. 64.

63 H.A. Alexander, 'Education in the Jewish state', *Studies in Philosophy and Education*, vol. 19, 2000, p. 504.

64 Henry, 'Education, Queer Theology', p. 8. Importantly, however, Henry cautions against the language of 'hospitality' that some of the literature on inclusive faith schooling slips into. This language presumes that there is a fixed religious (Jewish, Catholic, Muslim, Buddhist) norm which paternalistically accommodates the queer or religious other.

65 Connolly, *Pluralism*.

66 Connolly, *Pluralism*, pp. 42–43.

67 M. Lloyd, 'Hate, Loathing and Political Theory', in A. Finlayson (ed.), Democracy and Pluralism (London: Routledge, 2010), p. 115.

68 Alexander, Reimagining Liberal Education, p. 95.

2. Contested, Unchosen School Publics

1 K. Lynch and M. Moran, 'Markets, Schools and the Convertibility of Capital', British Journal of Sociology of Education, vol. 27, 2006, pp. 221–235.

2 Burman, 'Deconstructing Neoliberal Childhood'; Rizvi and Lingard, 'Social Equity'; Kitching, 'A Thousand Tiny Pluralities'.

3 Devine, Immigration and Schooling; E. Smyth, M. Darmody, M. Lyons, K. Lynch and E. Howlett, 'Children's Agency and Religious Identity in Irish Primary Schools', in Smyth et al., Religious Education, pp. 101–131.

4 Alexander, Reimagining Liberal Education, p. 87.

5 Organisation for Security and Co-operation in Europe Office for Democratic Institutions and Human Rights, Toledo Guiding Principles on Teaching About Religions and Beliefs in Public Schools (Warsaw: OSCE/ODIHR, 2007).

6 Weisse, 'RedCo'.

7 Alexander, Reimagining Liberal Education, p. 93.

8 L. Gearon, 'European Religious Education and European Civil Religion', British Journal of Educational Studies, vol. 60, 2012, pp. 151–169.

9 P. Hemming, Religion in the Primary School: Ethos, Diversity, Citizenship (London: Routledge, 2015), p. 117.

10 Hemming, Religion, pp. 125–126.

11 Equate Ireland, Religion and School.

12 A. Williams, P. Cloke and S. Thomas, 'Co-constituting Neoliberalism', Environment and Planning, vol. 44, 2012, pp. 1479–1501; K.N. Gulson and P.T. Webb, 'Education Policy Racialisations', Journal of Education Policy, vol. 27, 2013, pp. 697–709.

13 Asad, Formations of the Secular.

14 Dilger, 'Religion and the Formation of an Urban Educational Market'; Gulson and Webb, 'Education Policy Racialisations'; K.N. Gulson and P.T. Webb, "We Had to Hide We're Muslim', Discourse: Studies in the Cultural Politics of Education, vol. 34, 2013, pp. 628–641; K. Kitching, 'Governing "Authentic" Religiosity?', Irish Journal of Sociology, vol. 21, 2013, pp. 17–34.

15 G. Levy and M. Massalha, 'Yaffa: A School of their Choice?', British Journal of Sociology of Education, vol. 31, 2010 pp. 171–183.

16 Gulson and Webb, 'Education Policy Racialisations' and 'We Had to Hide We're Muslim'.

17 C. Byrne, 'Religion, the Elephant in the Asia-focused School Room', in L.G. Beaman and L. Van Arragon (eds), *Issues in Religious Education: Whose Religion?* (Leiden: Brill, 2015), pp. 257–281; C.A. MacGregor and B. Fitzpatrick, 'Catholic Schools in the Aftermath of Hurricane Katrina', in L. Mirón, B.R. Beabout and J.L. Boselovic (eds), *Only in New Orleans* (Rotterdam: Sense, 2015), pp. 37–52.

18 Coolahan et al., *The Forum on Patronage*.

19 O'Mahony, *Religious and Secular Places*, p. 33.

20 P. McGarry, 'Efforts to Divest Schools "Disappointing", Says Forum Chairman', *The Irish Times*, 10 November 2015.

21 S. Murray, 'New Schools Plan "Will Reflect More Diversity in 21st Century Ireland"', thejournal.ie, 30 January 2017.

22 I. McGimpsey, 'Late Neoliberalism', *Critical Social Policy*, vol. 37, 2017, pp. 64–84.

23 Department of Education and Skills, *Report for New Schools Establishment Group* (Dublin: Department of Education and Skills), p. 5.

24 A. Bryan, 'Corporate Multiculturalism, Diversity Management and Positive Interculturalism in Irish Schools and Society', *Irish Educational Studies*, vol. 29, 2010, pp. 253–269.

25 Classification of socio-economic disadvantage is based on participating schools being part of the state Delivering Equality of Opportunity in Schools (DEIS) scheme. Although one of the schools was in DEIS Band 1 and the other in DEIS Band 2 (Band 1 being designated the most disadvantaged), I have deliberately avoided attaching the specific DEIS band to each school.

26 International readers may wish to note the Church of Ireland refers to Anglican or Episcopalian Churches.

27 L. Fortunati and S. Taipale, 'Mobilities and the Network of Personal Technologies', *Telematics and Informatics*, vol. 34, 2017, pp. 560–568.

28 C. Holdsworth, *Family and Intimate Mobilities* (Hampshire: Palgrave MacMillan, 2013).

29 Darmody et al., *School Sector Variation*.

30 O'Mahony, *Secular and Religious Places*.

31 M. Scott, E. Murphy and M. Gkartzios, 'Placing "Home" and "Family" in Rural Residential Mobilities', *Sociologa Ruralis*, vol. 57, pp. 598–621.

32 Camogie is a GAA (Gaelic Athletic Association) sport specifically played by girls and women.

33 Scott et al., 'Placing "Home"'.

34 O'Mahony, *Secular and Religious Places*.

35 Darmody et al., *School Sector Variation*.

36 Amin, 'Ethnicity and the Multicultural City', p. 969.

37 D. Cohen, 'Market Mobilities/Immobilities', *Critical Studies in Education*, vol. 58, 2017, pp. 168–186.

3. Children, Worldviews and Plurality

1   O. Jones, '"True Geography [ ] Quickly Forgotten, Giving Away to an Adult-Imagined Universe"', *Children's Geographies*, vol. 6, pp. 195–212, 2008, p. 197.
2   Davis, 'Religion, Education', pp. 21–22.
3   Davis, 'Religion, Education', p. 24.
4   Our childhoods were differently experienced for many reasons of course – differing generational contexts, and different approaches to Catholicism, but perhaps more, different ethnicities and social classes, through which I experience(d) significantly greater privileges.
5   Davies, *Listening to Children*.
6   Davies, *Listening to Children*.
7   M. Hayse, 'Transcendence', in M.J.P. Wolf and B. Perron (ed.), *The Routledge Companion to Video Game Studies* (London: Routledge, 2014), p. 493.
8   D. Jackson, *Exploring Aging Masculinities: The Body, Sexuality and Social Lives* (Basingstoke: Palgrave Macmillan, 2016).
9   This theme is explored in more detail in chapter five, with reference to the competing values children negotiate.
10 *The White Dress* was directed by Niamh Gildea and produced by David Lawless for Brazen films. Virtually dialogue-free, it portrays an unnamed girl who lives in an inner-city high-rise flat, who moves entirely alone through her first communion day. Children's perspectives on the ethics of this are discussed in the next chapter, and the issue of clothing for a special day like first communion is discussed in the next section.
11 Kitching, 'A Thousand Tiny Pluralities'.
12 McGrail, *First Communion*, p. 13, [my parentheses and ellipses].
13 K. Kitching, 'An Excavation of the Racialised Politics of Viability Underpinning Education Policy in Ireland', *Irish Educational Studies,* vol. 29, 2010, pp. 213–229; Kitching, *Compulsive Education*.
14 *Irish Independent*, 'Hanafin Shocked by Communion "Brides"', 26 May 2009, my parentheses.
15 K. Kitching, 'What the Communion Season Tells Us about Irish Society'.
16 B. Skeggs and H. Wood, *Reacting to Reality Television* (London: Routledge, 2012.)
17 'Make more money' is a reference to the tradition of children receiving money as a Communion coming-of-age gift.
18 Hickey-Moody, 'Deleuze's Children', p. 282.

19 K. Sheridan, 'The First Holy Conundrum', *The Irish Times*, 12 May 2012; D. Ging, E. Kiely, K. Kitching and M. Leane, '#Slane Girl, Beauty Pageants and Padded Bras', *Feminist Media Studies, online edition*, 2018.

20 J. Ringrose and E. Renold, 'Teen Girls, Working-Class Femininity and Resistance: Retheorising Fantasy and Desire in Educational Contexts of Heterosexualised Violence', *International Journal of Inclusive Education*, vol. 16, 2012, pp. 461–477, p. 464, my parentheses.

21 Davis, 'Religion, Education'; Rasmussen, *'Progressive' Sexuality Education*.

22 S. Coakley, *Powers and Submissions: Spirituality, Philosophy and Gender* (Oxford: Blackwell, 2002).

23 McGrail, *First Communion*. The sacrament of communion is centred around the body of Jesus Christ. Celebration of the eucharist (a Greek term meaning 'thanksgiving') recalls Christ's command at the Last Supper to remember his sacrifice for the world. Catholic and Eastern Orthodox Churches view the bread and wine that is consecrated, or specially blessed, during the Mass as the actual body and blood of Christ, in an act known as transubstantiation. Anglican Churches vary on this interpretation. Indeed, so did some of the Catholic children participating in this study.

4. What Matters?

1 N. Ansell, 'Childhood and the Politics of Scale', *Progress in Human Geography*, vol. 33, 2009, pp. 190–209; P. Ariès, *Centuries of Childhood* (New York: Random House, 1962).

2 Mahmood, 'Religious Reason'.

3 Zelizer, Pricing the Priceless Child; Devine, '"Value"ing Migrant Children Differently?'

4 G. Deleuze, *Spinoza: Practical Philosophy*, translated by R. Hurley (San Francisco: City Lights Books, 1988); Braidotti, *Transpositions*.

5 Braidotti, *Transpositions*, pp. 148–151.

6 Braidotti, *Transpositions*, pp. 148-151.

7 Irish Episcopal Conference, *Catholic Preschool and Primary Religious Education Curriculum for Ireland* (Dublin: Veritas, 2015).

8 Hickey-Moody, 'Little Public Spheres'.

9 Chloe referenced 'skyscraper' churches and, later in this chapter, Cormac, who is non-religious, refers to the inaccessibility of churches for children.

10 Ansell, 'Childhood', p. 201.

11 Telecom Éireann was the Irish state's public telecoms company. It was privatised and renamed as Eircom in 1999.

12 The homeware company itself went entirely unremarked upon by the participating children.

13 Kitching, *Compulsive Education*.

14 S. Gillborn, B. Rickett, T. Muskett and M. Woolhouse, 'Apocalyptic Public Health', *Journal of Education Policy*, online edition. https://doi.org/10.10 80/02680939.2019.1566839.

15 See www.preparingforlife.ie (correct as of 31 March 2019).

16 H.J. Bacon, 'Sin or Slim? Christian Morality and the Politics of Personal Choice in a Secular Commercial Weight Loss Setting', *Fieldwork in Religion*, vol. 8, pp. 92–109.

17 Health Service Executive, *Schools for Health in Ireland Framework for Developing a Health Promoting School*.

5. Remembering Childhood, Engaging Ghosts, Imagining School Futures

1 U. Beck, *Risk Society* (London: Sage, 1986).

2 Braidotti, *Transpositions*, p. 17.

3 Gordon, *Ghostly Matters*, pp. 63–64.

4 L.A. Coser, 'Introduction', in M. Halbwachs, *On Collective Memory* (Chicago: Chicago University Press, 1992).

5 J.K. Olick., V. Vinitzky-Seroussi and D. Levy, 'Introduction', in J.K. Olick, V. Vinitzky-Seroussi and D. Levy (eds), *The Collective Memory Reader* (Oxford: Oxford University Press, 2011), p. 10. Olick et al. state 'where people from different milieus congregate together in polyglot urban settings, leaving behind both their earlier contexts and to some degree their earlier selves, where the labors of life are more highly differentiated than in rural households . . . the basis of agreement and the bonds of commonality are much less obvious, requiring vast new efforts and conceptual frameworks'.

6 O. Jones, 'Endlessly Revisited and Forever Gone', *Children's Geographies*, vol. 1, 2003, p. 30.

7 L.A. Coser, The Revival of the Sociology of Culture', *Sociological Forum*, vol. 7, 1992, pp. 365–373; B. Schwartz, 'The Social Context of Commemoration', *Social Forces*, vol. 61, 1982, pp. 374–402.

8 U. Neisser, 'Five Kinds of Self-Narratives', *Philosophical Psychology*, vol. 1, 1988, pp. 35–59. Neisser presents the *ecological* self as that which is perceived, optically, sensorily etc. from earliest infancy with respect to the material environment ('I' am the embodied person here in this place, engaged in this activity); the *interpersonal* self is specified by expressive signals of emotional rapport and communication; the *extended* self is based primarily on our personal memories and anticipations, that is, it is the self as it was in the past and as we expect it to be in the future,

'known primarily on the basis of memory'; the *private* self appears when children first notice some of their experiences are not directly shared with others (for example, 'I am in principle the only one who can feel this unique, particular pain'); and the *conceptual* self or self-concept, which draws its meaning from a network of assumptions and theories it is embedded in, for example, social roles (father, teacher), internal entities (soul, unconscious mind, brain), and dimensions of difference (wealth, attractiveness, etc.). These selves are indivisible – self-concept, for example, mediates the extended/remembered self. Each kind of self-knowledge has different developmental trajectories 'in what we know about them, in the pathologies to which they are subject, and in the manner they contribute to human social experience'. A pathology particular to the extended self is amnesia.

9   U. Neisser, 'Self-Narratives: True and False', in U. Neisser and R. Fivush (eds), *The Remembering Self: Construction and Accuracy in the Self-Narrative* (Cambridge: Cambridge University Press, 1994). Neisser argues it is *because,* not in spite of, the importance of reconstruction and multiple histories and counter-histories that we cannot equivocate about what is remembered and what is forgotten: 'we must still *believe* that the past consisted of some definite set of events that have had specific consequences' (p. 1).

10 Bond Stockton, *The Queer Child*, pp. 5–6.

11 Maguire, *Precarious Childhood*.

12 Indeed, this exchange encapsulates a number of themes in this book: the deinstitutionalisation of Catholic identity (I'm a big believer, I don't go to Mass), how religiosity and religious material culture mediate happiness and pain (my holy picture, the image of the devil), the presence of diverse values and memories amongst those identifying as Catholic (Therese challenging Julie on purgatory, the effect of poverty on her views), the desire for social reproduction through children (eventually bringing her child to Mass).

13 K. Kitching, 'How the Irish Became CRT'd?' *Race Ethnicity and Education*, vol. 18, 2015, pp. 163–182.

14 Davis, 'Religion, Education'.

15 L. Godson, 'Catholicism and Material Culture in Ireland 1840–1880', *Circa,* vol. 103, 2003, pp. 38–45; 'Catholicism and Material Culture', p. 40. Despite a history of criticism from theologians, Catholic art reformers and, ultimately, the Vatican, about how such art would distract from the 'proper' focus of devotion (the Mass), the material legacy of secular–religious relations is visible, for example, in largely uncontested, publicly placed statues of the Virgin Mary.

16 McGrail, *First Communion*, p. 13.

17 S. Jansen, 'Hope and the State in the Anthropology of Home,' *Ethnologia Europaea. Journal of European Ethnology*, vol. 39, 2009, pp. 54–60.
18 Heinz, Davison and Keane, 'I Will Do it but Religion Is a Very Personal Thing'.
19 Holdsworth, *Family and Intimate Mobilities*, p. 22.
20 Alexander, *Reimagining Liberal Education*, p. 104.
21 Smith, 'Producing Governable Subjects'.
22 F. Gino and S.D. Desai, 'Memory Lane and Morality', *Journal of Personality and Social Psychology*, vol. 102, pp. 743–758. Gino and Desai contend that when they used experiments where participants were primed to remember positive and negative childhood events, they found a greater likelihood of remembering helping others, donating to a good cause, and punishing others for wrongdoing.
23 M. Halbwachs, 'The Collective Memory', in K. Olick, V. Vinitzky-Seroussi and D. Levy (eds), *The Collective Memory Reader* (Oxford: Oxford University Press, 2011), pp. 142–144.

6. Building Affirmative, Unchosen School Publics

1 Braidotti, *Transpositions*, p. 85.
2 A. Cavarero, *For More Than One Voice*, translated by P.A. Kottman (Stanford, CA: Stanford University Press, 2005), p. 89.
3 J. Butler, 'Sexual Politics, Torture and Secular Time', *The British Journal of Sociology*, vol. 59, 2008, pp. 1–23.
4 M.L. Rasmussen, *Progressive Sexuality Education: The Conceits of Secularism* (London: Routledge, 2015).
5 N. Fernando, 'The Discursive Violence of Postcolonial Asylum in the Irish Republic', *Postcolonial Studies*, vol. 19, 2016, pp. 393–408.
6 A. Mbembe, 'Necropolitics', translated by Libby Meintjes, *Public Culture*, vol. 15, 2003, pp. 11–40.
7 O'Mahony, *Secular and Religious Places*.
8 Gordon, *Ghostly Matters*, pp. 63–64.
9 Braidotti, 'Posthuman Affirmative Politics', p. 51.
10 Braidotti, 'Residual Spirituality', pp. 262–263.
11 Biesta, 'Becoming Public', p. 687; H. Arendt, *Between Past and Future: Eight Exercises in Political Thought* (Harmondsworth: Penguin Books, 1977).
12 Braidotti, *Transpositions*, pp. 148–151.
13 J. Butler, *Giving an Account of Oneself* (New York: Fordham University Press, 2005).
14 S. Mahmood, 'Feminist Theory, Agency and the Liberatory Subject: Some Reflections on the Islamic Revival in Egypt', *Temenos*, vol. 42, 2006, pp. 31–71.

15 Braidotti, 'Posthuman Affirmative Politics', p. 30.

16 Braidotti, 'Posthuman Affirmative Politics', pp. 30–31, my parentheses.

17 Kitching, *The Politics of Compulsive Education*.

18 Braidotti, 'Posthuman Affirmative Politics', p. 31.

19 H. Arendt, *The Human Condition* (Chicago: The University of Chicago Press, 1957), p. 57.

20 Braidotti, *Transpositions*, p. 17.

21 Hickey-Moody, 'Arts Practice'.

22 Coolahan et al., *The Forum on Patronage and Pluralism*, p. 13.

23 Bond Stockton, *The Queer Child*.

24 National Council for Curriculum and Assessment (NCCA), *Goodness Me, Goodness You! Curriculum for 3rd to 6th Class* (Dublin: NCCA, 2016), p. 3.

25 NCCA, *Education about Religions and Beliefs (ERB) and Ethics in the Primary School: Consultation Paper* (Dublin, NCCA, 2015).

26 M. Darmody and E. Smyth, *Education about Religions and Beliefs (ERB) and Ethics: Views of Teachers, Parents and the General Public Regarding the Proposed Curriculum for Primary Schools. Consultation Paper Prepared for the NCCA* (Dublin: Economic and Social Research Institute, 2017).

27 Darmody and Smyth, *Education about Religions and Beliefs*.

28 Darmody and Smyth, *Education about Religions and Beliefs*, p. 25.

29 Darmody and Smyth, *Education about Religions and Beliefs*, p. 38.

30 S. Todd, 'Educating Beyond Cultural Diversity', *Studies in Philosophy of Education*, vol. 30, 2011, pp. 101–111.

31 Todd, 'Educating Beyond Cultural Diversity', pp. 104–105.

32 Cavarero, *For More Than One Voice*.

33 ODIHR/OSCE, *Toledo Guiding Principles*, p. 16.

34 Braidotti, 'Residual Spirituality'.

35 Connolly, *Pluralism*, pp. 42–43.

36 Braidotti, *Transpositions*, p. 7.

37 I. Tyler, 'Classificatory Struggles', *The Sociological Review*, vol. 63, 2015, pp. 493–511; Kitching, 'A Thousand Tiny Pluralities'.

38 Bacon et al., *Alternative Salvations*. Ethical accountability to one another can involve theological notions of salvation, but in a way that rejects paternalistic attempts to 'save' Others and instead engage collective release, or reconciliation.

39 A. O'Donnell, P. Kieran, L. Bergdahl, S. Cherouvis and E. Langmann, *The Enquiring Classroom Conceptual and Pedagogical Framework* (2019), available at http://www.enquiring-project.eu/home.html (Last accessed 15 November 2019).

40 M. MacLure, 'The Refrain of the A-Grammatical Child', p. 179.

References

Alexander, H.A., 'Education in the Jewish State', *Studies in Philosophy and Education*, vol. 19, 2000, pp. 491–507

Alexander, H., *Reimagining Liberal Education: Affiliation and Inquiry in Democratic Schooling* (London: Bloomsbury, 2015)

Amin, A., 'Ethnicity and the Multicultural City: Living with Diversity', *Environment and Planning A*, vol. 34, 2002, pp. 959–980

Ansell, N., 'Childhood and the Politics of Scale: Descaling Children's Geographies?' *Progress in Human Geography*, vol. 33, 2009, pp. 190–209

Arendt, H., *Between Past and Future: Eight Exercises in Political Thought* (Harmondsworth: Penguin Books, 1977)

Ariès, P., *Centuries of Childhood: A Social History of Family Life* (New York: Random House, 1962)

Asad, T., *Formations of the Secular: Christianity, Islam, Modernity* (Stanford: Stanford University Press, 2003)

Asad, T., *Genealogies of Religion: Discipline and Reasons of Power in Christianity and Islam* (Baltimore, MA: John Hopkins University Press, 1993)

Association of Trustees of Catholic Schools, *A Guide to Patronage and Trusteeship of Catholic Schools in Ireland*, 2012. Available at https://www.catholicschools.ie/useful-publications/useful-publications-for-catholic-primary-schools/ (Last accessed 21 April 2019)

Bacon, H.J., 'Sin or Slim? Christian Morality and the Politics of Personal Choice in a Secular Commercial Weight Loss Setting', *Fieldwork in Religion*, vol. 8, pp. 92–109

Bacon, H., Dossett, W. and Knowles, S. (eds), *Alternative Salvations: Engaging the Sacred and the Secular* (New York: Bloomsbury, 2015)

Beck, U., *Risk Society: Towards a New Modernity* (London: Sage, 1986)

Beckford, J., *Cult Controversies: The Societal Response to New Religious Movements* (London: Tavistock, 1985)

Berglund, J., Shanneik, Y. and Bocking, B. (eds), *Religious Education in a Global-Local World* (Cham, Switzerland: Springer, 2016)

Bhambra, G.K., *Rethinking Modernity* (Basingstoke: Palgrave, 2007)

Bhambra, G.K., *Connected Sociologies* (London: Bloomsbury, 2014)

Bhattacharyya, G., 'Racial Neoliberal Britain?', in N. Kapoor, V.S. Kalra and J. Rhodes (eds), *The State of Race* (Basingstoke: Palgrave Macmillan, 2013), pp. 31–48

Biesta, G., 'Becoming Public: Public Pedagogy, Citizenship and the Public Sphere', *Social and Cultural Geography*, vol. 13, 2012, pp. 683–697

Bond Stockton, K., *The Queer Child, or Growing Sideways in the Twentieth Century* (Durham: Duke University Press, 2009)

Braidotti, R., 'Feminist Epistemology After Postmodernism', *Interdisciplinary Science Reviews*, vol. 32, 2007, pp. 65–74

Braidotti, R., *Nomadic Theory: The Portable Rosi Braidotti* (New York: Columbia University Press, 2011)

Braidotti, R., 'Posthuman Affirmative Politics', in S.E. Wilmer and A. Žukauskaitė (eds), *Resisting Biopolitics: Philosophical, Political and Performative Strategies* (London: Routledge, 2016), pp. 30–56

Braidotti, R., *Transpositions: On Nomadic Theory* (Cambridge: Polity, 2006)

Braidotti, R., 'The Residual Spirituality in Critical Theory', in R. Braidotti, B. Blaagaard, T. de Graauw and E. Midden (eds), *Transformations of Religion and the Public Sphere: Postsecular Publics* (Basingstoke: Palgrave Macmillan, 2014), pp. 249–272

Braidotti, R., Blaagaard, B., de Graaauw, T. and Midden, E., 'Introductory Notes', in R. Braidotti, B. Blaagaard, T. de Graauw and E. Midden (eds), *Transformations of Religion and the Public Sphere: Postsecular Publics* (Basingstoke: Palgrave Macmillan, 2014), pp. 1–13

Bruce, S., 'Religion and Rational Choice: A Critique of Economic Explanations of Religious Behaviour', *Sociology of Religion*, vol. 54, 1993, pp. 193–205

Bryan, A., 'Corporate Multiculturalism, Diversity Management and Positive Interculturalism in Irish Schools and Society', *Irish Educational Studies*, vol. 29, 2010, pp. 253–269

Burman, E., 'Brexit, "Child as Method", and the Pedagogy of Failure', *Review of Education, Pedagogy and Culture*, vol. 40, 2018, pp. 119–143

Burman, E., 'Deconstructing Neoliberal Childhood: Towards a Feminist Antipsychological Approach', *Childhood*, vol. 19, 2011, pp. 423–438

Burman, E., *Developments: Child, Image, Nation* (Routledge: London, 2008)

Butler, J., *Giving an Account of Oneself* (New York: Fordham University Press, 2005)

Butler, J., 'Sexual Politics, Torture and Secular Time', *The British Journal of Sociology*, vol. 59, 2008, pp. 1–23

Butler, J., *Undoing Gender* (London: Routledge, 2004)

Byrne, .C., 'Religion, the Elephant in the Asia-focused School Room', in L.G. Beaman and L. Van Arragon (eds), *Issues in Religious Education: Whose Religion?* (Leiden: Brill, 2015), pp. 257–281

Byrne, G., and Kieran, P. (eds), *Toward Mutual Ground: Pluralism, Religious Education and Diversity in Irish Schools* (Dublin: The Columba Press, 2013)

Byrne, R. and Devine, D., 'Catholic Schooling with a Twist? A Study of Faith Schooling in the Republic of Ireland during a Period of Detraditionalisation', *Cambridge Journal of Education*, vol. 48, 2018, pp. 461–477

Carr, J., *Experiences of Islamophobia*: *Living with Racism in the Neoliberal Era* (London: Routledge, 2016)

Catholic Schools Partnership, *Catholic Primary Schools in a Changing Ireland*: *Sharing Good Practice on Inclusion of All Pupils* (Maynooth: Catholic Schools Partnership, 2015)

Cavarero, A., *For More Than One Voice*, translated by P.A. Kottman (Stanford, CA: Stanford University Press)

Chandhoke, N., *Rethinking Pluralism, Secularism and Tolerance: Anxieties of Coexistence* (London: Sage, 2019)

Chryssides, G.D. and Wilkins, M.Z., *A Reader in New Religious Movements: Readings in the Study of Religious Movements* (London: Continuum, 2006)

Coakley, S., *Powers and Submissions: Spirituality, Philosophy and Gender* (Oxford: Blackwell, 2002)

Cohen, D., 'Market Mobilities/Immobilities: Mutation, Path-Dependency, and the Spread of Charter School Policies in the United States', *Critical Studies in Education*, vol. 58, pp. 168–186

Connolly, W. E., *Pluralism* (Durham: Duke University Press, 2005)

Cooey, P. M., 'Neither Seen nor Heard: The Absent Child in the Study of Religion', *Journal of Childhood and Religion*, vol. 1, 2010, pp. 1–31

Coolahan, J., Hussey, C. and Kilfeather, P., *The Forum on Patronage and Pluralism in the Primary Sector: Report of the Forum's Advisory Group* (Dublin: Department of Education and Skills)

Coser, L.A., 'Introduction', in M. Halbwachs, *On Collective Memory* (Chicago: Chicago University Press, 1992)

Coser, L.A., 'The Revival of the Sociology of Culture: The Case of Collective Memory', *Sociological Forum*, vol. 7, 1992, pp. 365–373

Crenshaw, K., 'Mapping the Margins: Intersectionality, Identity Politics and Violence against Women of Color', *Stanford Law Review*, vol. 43, 1991, pp. 1241–1299

Dahlberg, G. and Moss, P., *Ethics and Politics in Early Childhood Education* (London: Routledge/Falmer, 2005)

Daly, E., *Religion, Law and the Irish State* (Dublin: Clarus Press, 2012)

Darmody, M., Smyth, E. and McCoy, S., *School Sector Variation Among Primary Schools in Ireland* (Dublin: ESRI and Educate Together, 2012)

Darmody, M. and Smyth, E., *Education about Religions and Beliefs (ERB) and Ethics: Views of Teachers, Parents and the General Public Regarding the Proposed Curriculum for Primary Schools. Consultation Paper Prepared for the NCCA* (Dublin: Economic and Social Research Institute, 2017)

Davies, B., *Listening to Children: Being and Becoming* (London: Routledge, 2014)

Davis, R.A., 'Religion, Education and the Post-Secular Child', *Critical Studies in Education*, vol. 55, pp. 18–31

De Sousa Santos, B., '*Nuestra America*: Reinventing a Subaltern Paradigm of Recognition and Redistribution', *Theory, Culture and Society*, vol. 18, 185–217

Deegan, J., Devine, D. and Lodge, A. (eds), *Primary Voices: Equality, Diversity and Childhood in Irish Primary Schools* (Dublin: Institute of Public Administration, 2004)

Delay, C., 'Holy Water and a Twig: Catholic Households and Women's Religious Authority in Modern Ireland', *Journal of Family History,* vol. 43, 2018, pp. 302–319

Deleuze, G., *Spinoza: Practical Philosophy*, translated by R. Hurley (San Francisco: City Lights Books, 1988)

Department of Education and Skills, *Key Statistics 2016/2017 and 2017/2018* (Dublin: Government Stationery Office, 2018)

Department of Education and Skills, *Report for New Schools Establishment Group: Patronage for New Primary Schools for September 2017 & 2018* (Dublin: DES, 2018)

Devine, D., *Immigration and Schooling in the Republic of Ireland: Making a Difference?* (Manchester: Manchester University Press, 2011)

Devine, D., '"Value"ing Migrant Children Differently? Migrant Children in Education', *Children and Society*, vol. 27, 2013, pp. 282–294

Duffy, M., 'Affect and Emotion in Children's Place-Making', in T. Skelton, K. Nairn and P. Kraftl (eds), *Space, Place and Environment* (Singapore: Springer, 2016), pp. 379–400

Equate Ireland, *Religion and School: Parents' Voices* (Dublin: Equate Ireland, 2017)

Faas, D., Smith, A., and Darmody, M., 'Children's Agency in Multi-Belief Settings: The Case of Community National Schools in Ireland', *Journal of Research in Childhood Education*, vol. 32, 2018, pp. 486–500

Fanning, B., 'A Catholic Vision of Ireland', in T. Inglis (ed), *Are the Irish Different?* (Manchester: Manchester University Press, 2014), pp. 44–53

Fendler, L., 'Educating Flexible Souls: The Construction of Subjectivity through Developmentality and Interaction, in K. Hultqvist and G. Dahlberg (eds), *Governing the Child in the New Millennium* (London: Routledge Falmer, 2001), pp. 119–142

Finlayson, A., 'Introduction: Becoming Plural', in A. Finlayson (ed), *Democracy and Pluralism: The Political Thought of William E. Connolly* (London: Routledge, 2010)

Fischer, K., *Schools and the Politics of Religion and Diversity in the Republic of Ireland: Separate but Equal?* (Manchester: Manchester University Press, 2016)

Folgerø, T., 'Queer Nuclear Families? Reproducing and Transgressing Homonormativity', *Journal of Homosexuality*, vol. 54, 2008, pp. 121–149

Fortunati, L. and Taipale, S., 'Mobilities and the Network of Personal Technologies: Refining the Understanding of Mobility Structure', *Telematics and Informatics*, vol. 34, 2017, pp. 560–568

Fraser, N., 'Rethinking the Public Sphere: A Contribution to the Critique of Actually Existing Democracy', *Social Text*, vol. 25/26, 1990, pp. 56–80

Garrattini, C., 'Creating Memories: Material Culture and Infantile Death in Contemporary Ireland', *Mortality*, vol. 12, 2007, pp. 193–206

Gearon, L., 'European Religious Education and European Civil Religion', *British Journal of Educational Studies*, vol. 60, 2012, pp. 151–169

Gillborn, S., Rickett, B., Muskett, T. and Woolhouse, M., 'Apocalyptic Public Health: Exploring Discourses of Fatness in Childhood "Obesity Policy"', *Journal of Education Policy,* online edition https://doi.org/10.1080/02680939.2019.1566839

Ging, D., Kiely, E., Kitching, K. and Leane, M., '#Slane Girl, Beauty Pageants and Padded Bras: Flashpoints in the Sexualisation of Children Debate in Irish Media and Political Discourse', *Feminist Media Studies,* online edition, 2018

Gino, F. and Desai, S.D., 'Memory Lane and Morality: How Childhood Memories Promote Prosocial Behaviour', *Journal of Personality and Social Psychology*, vol. 102, pp. 743–758

Godson, L., 'Catholicism and Material Culture in Ireland 1840–1880', *Circa,* vol. 103, 2003, pp. 38–45

Gordon, A.F., *Ghostly Matters: Haunting and the Sociological Imagination* (Minneapolis: University of Minnesota Press, 2008)

Gulson, K.N. and Webb, P.T., 'Education Policy Racialisations: Afrocentric Schools, Islamic Schools, and the New Enunciations of Equity', *Journal of Education Policy*, vol. 27, 2013, pp. 697–709

Gulson, K.N. and Webb, P.T., '"We Had to Hide We're Muslim": Ambient Fear, Islamic Schools and the Geographies of Race and Religion', *Discourse: Studies in the Cultural Politics of Education*, vol. 34, 2013, pp. 628–641

Hage, G., *Alter-Politics: Critical Anthropology and the Radical Imagination* (Melbourne: Melbourne University Press, 2015)

Halberstam, J., 'Justifiable Matricide: Backlashing Faludi'. Available at https://bullybloggers.wordpress.com/2010/10/19/justifiable-matricide-backlashing-faludi-by-jack-halberstam/

Halbwachs, M., 'The Collective Memory', in K. Olick, V. Vinitzky-Seroussi and D. Levy (eds), *The Collective Memory Reader* (Oxford: Oxford University Press, 2011)

Hayse, M., 'Transcendence', in M.J.P. Wolf and B. Perron (eds), *The Routledge Companion to Video Game Studies* (London: Routledge, 2014), pp. 493–501

Heinz, M., Davison, K. and Keane, E., 'I Will Do it but Religion is a Very Personal Thing', *European Journal of Teacher Education*, vol. 41, 2018, pp. 232–245

Hemming, P., 'Educating for Religious Citizenship: Multiculturalism and National Identity in an English Multi-Faith Primary School', *Transactions of the Institute of British Geographers*, vol. 36, 2011, pp. 441–454

Hemming, P., *Religion in the Primary School: Ethos, Diversity, Citizenship* (London: Routledge, 2015)

Henry, S., 'Education, Queer Theology and Spiritual Development: Disrupting Heteronormativity for Inclusion in Jewish, Muslim and Christian Faith Schools', *International Journal of Children's Spirituality*, vol. 23, 2018, pp. 3–16

Hickey-Moody, A., 'Little Public Spheres', *Performance Paradigm: A Journal of Performance and Contemporary Culture*, vol. 9, 2013, https://www.performanceparadigm.net/wp-content/uploads/2013/08/hickey-moody-anna-little-public-spheres.pdf

Hickey-Moody, A.C., 'Arts Practice as Method, Urban Spaces and Intra-active Faiths', *International Journal of Inclusive Education*, vol. 21, 2017, pp. 1083–1096

Hickey-Moody, A.C., 'Deleuze's Children', *Educational Philosophy and Theory*, vol. 45, 2013, pp. 272–286

Holdsworth, C., *Family and Intimate Mobilities* (Hampshire: Palgrave MacMillan, 2013)

Houtman, D. and S. Aupers, 'The Spiritual Turn and the Decline of Tradition: The Spread of Post-Christian Spirituality in 14 Countries, 1981–2000', *Journal for the Scientific Study of Religion*, vol. 46, 2007, pp. 305–320

Hyman, G., 'Atheism in Modern History', in M. Martin (ed.), *The Cambridge Companion to Atheism* (Cambridge: Cambridge University Press, 2007), pp. 27–46

Inglis, T., 'The Global and the Local: Mapping Changes in Irish Childhood', *Éire-Ireland*, vol. 46, 2011, pp. 1–21

Inglis, T., 'Catholic Identity in Contemporary Ireland: Belief and Belonging to Tradition', *Journal of Contemporary Religion*, vol. 22, 2007, pp. 205–220

Inglis, T., *Moral Monopoly: The Rise and Fall of the Catholic Church in Modern Ireland* (Dublin: University College Dublin Press, 1998)

Irish Episcopal Conference, *Catholic Preschool and Primary Religious Education Curriculum for Ireland* (Dublin: Veritas, 2015)

Irish Independent, 'Hanafin Shocked by Communion "Brides"', 26 May 2009, https://www.independent.ie/irish-news/hanafin-shocked-by-communion-brides-26538899.html

Irwin, J., 'Existential Thought between Ethics and Religion as Related to Curriculum: From Kierkegaard to Sartre', in Shanahan, M. (ed), *Does Religious Education Matter?* (Abingdon: Routledge, 2017)

Isin, E.F. and Nielsen, G.M., 'Introduction', in E.F. Isin, and G.M. Nielsen (eds), *Acts of Citizenship* (London: Zed Books, 2008), pp. 1–12

Jackson, D., *Exploring Aging Masculinities: The Body, Sexuality and Social Lives* (Basingstoke: Palgrave MacMillan, 2016)

Jansen, S., 'Hope and the State in the Anthropology of Home: Preliminary Notes', *Ethnologia Europaea. Journal of European Ethnology*, vol. 39, 2009, pp. 54–60

Jones, O., '"Endlessly Revisited and Forever Gone": On Memory, Reverie and Emotional Imagination in Doing Children's Geographies. An "Addendum" to "'To Go Back up the Side Hill': Memories, Imaginations and Reveries of Childhood" by Chris Philo', *Children's Geographies*, vol. 1, 2003, pp. 25–36

Jones, O., 'True Geography [ ] Quickly Forgotten, Giving Away to an Adult-Imagined Universe: Approaching the Otherness of Childhood'. *Children's Geographies*, vol. 6, 2008, pp. 195–212

Kieran, P., 'Taking Diversity of Belief Seriously in Contemporary Ireland', in G. Byrne and P. Kieran (eds), *Toward Mutual Ground* (Dublin: The Columba Press, 2013), pp. 23–39

Kitching, K., 'A Thousand Tiny Pluralities', *Critical Studies in Education*, online edition, 2017

Kitching, K., 'Governing "Authentic" Religiosity? The Responsibilisation of Parents Beyond Religion and State in Matters of School Ethos in Ireland', *Irish Journal of Sociology*, vol. 21, 2013, pp. 17–34

Kitching, K., 'How the Irish Became CRT'd? "Greening" Critical Race Theory and the Pitfalls of a Normative Atlantic State View', *Race Ethnicity and Education*, vol. 18, 2015, pp. 163–182

Kitching, K., *The Politics of Compulsive Education: Racism and Learner-Citizenship* (London: Routledge, 2014)

Kitching, K. and Shanneik, Y., *Children's Beliefs and Belongings: A Schools and Families Report from the 'Making Communion' Study* (Cork: Authors, 2015)

246

Kong, L., 'Mapping "New" Geographies of Religion: Politics and Poetics of Modernity', *Progress in Human Geography*, vol. 25, 2001, pp. 211–233

Kong, L., 'Religious Schools: For Spirit, (F)or Nation', *Environment and Planning D: Society and Space*, vol. 23, 2005, pp. 615–631

Larkin, E., 'The Devotional Revolution in Ireland, 1850–75', *American Historical Review*, vol. 77, pp. 625–652

Lentin, A. and Titley, G., *The Crises of Multiculturalism: Racism in a Neoliberal Age* (London: Zed Books, 2011)

Lenz Taguchi, H., *Going Beyond the Theory/Practice Divide in Early Childhood Education: Introducing an Intra-Active Pedagogy* (London: Routledge/Falmer, 2010)

Levy, G. and Massalha, M., 'Yaffa: A School of their Choice?', *British Journal of Sociology of Education*, vol. 31, 2010, pp. 171–183

Lloyd, M., 'Hate, Loathing and Political Theory', in A. Finlayson (ed.), *Democracy and Pluralism: The Political Thought of William E. Connolly* (London: Routledge, 2010), p. 115

Lodge, A., 'First Communion in Carnduffy: A Religious and Secular Rite of Passage', *Irish Educational Studies*, vol. 18, pp. 210–222

Lynch, K. and Moran, M., 'Markets, Schools and the Convertibility of Capital: The Complex Dynamics of Class Choice', *British Journal of Sociology of Education*, vol. 27, 2006, pp. 221–235

MacLure, M., 'The Refrain of the A-Grammatical Child: Finding Another Language in/for Qualitative Research', *Cultural Studies – Critical Methodologies*, vol. 16, 2016, pp. 173–182

Maguire, M.J., *Precarious Childhood in Post-Independence Ireland* (Manchester: Manchester University Press, 2009)

Mahmood, S., 'Feminist Theory, Agency and the Liberatory Subject: Some Reflections on the Islamic Revival in Egypt', *Temenos*, vol. 42, 2006, pp. 31–71

Mahmood, S., 'Religious Reason and Secular Affect: An Incommensurable Divide?' *Critical Inquiry*, vol. 35, 2009, pp. 836–862

Malesevic, V., 'Ireland and Neo-Secularisation Theory', *Irish Journal of Sociology*, vol. 18, 2010, 22–42

Mawhinney, A., *Freedom of Religion and Schools: The Case of Ireland* (Saarbrücken: VDM Verlag, 2009)

McDannell, C., *Material Christianity, Religion and Popular Culture in America* (London: Yale University Press, 1995)

McGarry, P., 'Efforts to Divest Schools "Disappointing", Says Forum Chairman', *The Irish Times*, 10 November 2015

McGrail, P., *First Communion: Ritual, Church and Popular Religious Identity* (Aldershot: Ashgate, 2007), p. 169

McGrath, T., 'The Tridentine Evolution of Modern Irish Catholicism', in R. Ó Muirí (ed.), *Irish Church History Today* (Armagh: Cumann Seanchais Ard Mhacha, 1991), pp. 84–99

MacGregor, C.A. and Fitzpatrick, B., 'Catholic Schools in the Aftermath of Hurricane Katrina', in L. Mirón, B.R. Beabout and J.L. Boselovic (eds), *Only in New Orleans*: *School Choice and Equity Post-Hurricane Katrina* (Rotterdam: Sense, 2015), pp. 37–52

McGimpsey, I., 'Late Neoliberalism: Delineating a Policy Regime', *Critical Social Policy*, vol. 37, 2017, pp. 64–84

Meaney, G., 'Race, Sex and Nation', *The Irish Review*, vol. 35, 2007, pp. 46–63

Miller, V., *Consuming Religion: Christian Faith and Practice in a Consumer Culture* (London: Bloomsbury, 2005)

Murray, S., 'New Schools Plan "Will Reflect More Diversity in 21st Century Ireland"', thejournal.ie, 30 January 2017. Available at https://www.thejournal.ie/bruton-denominational-schools-3212288-Jan2017/ (Last accessed 22 April 2019)

Neary, A., *LGBT-Q Teachers, Civil Partnership and Same-Sex Marriage* (London: Routledge, 2017)

Neisser, U., 'Five Kinds of Self-Narratives', *Philosophical Psychology*, vol. 1, 1988, pp. 35–59

Neisser, U., 'Self-Narratives: True and False', in U. Neisser and R. Fivush (eds), *The Remembering Self: Construction and Accuracy in the Self-Narrative* (Cambridge: Cambridge University Press, 1994), pp. 1–18

Nixon, A.G., *New Atheism as a Case of Competitive Postsecular Worldviews*. Doctoral thesis, University of Western Sydney, 2014

Nye, M., *Religion: The Basics*, 2nd Edition (London: Routledge, 2008)

O'Donnell, A., Kieran, P., Bergdahl, L., Cherouvis, S., and Langmann, E., *The Enquiring Classroom Conceptual and Pedagogical Framework* (2019). Available at http://www.enquiring-project.eu/home.html (Last accessed 21 April 2019)

O'Driscoll, K., *Reform, Instruction and Practice: The Impact of the Catholic Revival on the Laity in the Dublin Diocese, 1793–1853*. PhD Thesis, NUI Galway, 2016

O'Kelly, E., 'Parents Need to Make Informed Choices over School Patronage', RTÉ News, 3 April 2019. Available at https://www.rte.ie/news/analysis-and-comment/2019/0403/1040338-school-patronage/ (Last accessed 3 April 2019)

O'Kelly, E., 'Third Dublin School Sends Letter Warning of Consequences over Changing Patronage', RTÉ News, 3 April 2019. Available at https://www.rte.ie/news/2019/0403/1040323-school_patronage/ (Last accessed 16 November 2019)

O'Mahony, E., *Factors Determining School Choice: Report on a Survey of the Attitudes of Parents of Children Attending Catholic Primary Schools in Ireland* (Maynooth: Irish Catholic Bishop's Conference, 2008)

O'Mahony, E., *Religious and Secular Places: Understanding the Changing Geographies of Religion in Ireland*. PhD thesis, National University of Ireland Maynooth, 2015

O'Sullivan, D., *Cultural Politics and Irish Education Since the 1950s: Policy Paradigms and Power* (Dublin: Institute of Public Administration, 2005)

Olick, J.K., Vinitzky-Seroussi, V. and Levy, D., 'Introduction', in J.K. Olick, V. Vinitzky-Seroussi and D. Levy (eds), *The Collective Memory Reader* (Oxford: Oxford University Press, 2011), pp. 3–62

Organisation for Security and Co-operation in Europe Office for Democratic Institutions and Human Rights, *Toledo Guiding Principles on Teaching About Religions and Beliefs in Public Schools* (Warsaw: OSCE/ODIHR, 2007)

Pellandini-Simányi, L., 'Bourdieu, Ethics and Symbolic Power', *The Sociological Review*, vol. 62, 2014, pp. 651–674

Pew Research Centre, *Being Christian in Western Europe* (Pew Research Centre, 2018). Available at https://www.pewforum.org/2018/05/29/being-christian-in-western-europe/ (Last accessed 3 April 2019)

Pierce, J., Martin, D.G. and Murphy, J.T., 'Relational Place-Making: The Networked Politics of Place', *Transactions of the Institute of British Geographers,* vol. 36, 2011, pp. 54–70

Qvortrup, J., 'Varieties of Childhood', in J. Qvortrup (ed.), *Studies in Modern Childhood* (Hampshire: Palgrave Macmillan, 2005), pp. 1–20

Rasmussen, M.L., *'Progressive' Sexuality Education: The Conceits of Secularism* (London: Routledge, 2015)

Reid, G., Bridigi, P., Burton, J.P., Contractor, N., Duncan, S., Fargier, E., Hill, C., Lebeer, S., Martín, R., McBain, A.J., Mor, G., O'Neill, C., Rodríguez, J.M., Swann, J., van Hermert, S. and Ansell, J., 'Microbes Central to Human Reproduction', *American Journal of Reproductive Immunology*, vol. 73, 2014, pp. 1–11

Renold, E., Ringrose, J. and Egan, R.D. (eds), *Children, Sexuality and Sexualization* (Hampshire: Palgrave Macmillan, 2015)

Ridgley Bales, S., *When I Was a Child: Children's Interpretations of First Communion* (North Carolina: The University of North Carolina Press, 2005)

Ringrose, J., and Renold, E., 'Teen Girls, Working-Class Femininity and Resistance: Retheorising Fantasy and Desire in Educational Contexts of Heterosexualised Violence', *International Journal of Inclusive Education*, vol. 16, 2012, pp. 461–477

Rizvi, A.A., *The Atheist Muslim: A Journey from Religion to Reason* (New York: St Martin's Press, 2017)

Rizvi, F. and Lingard, B., 'Social Equity and the Assemblage of Values in Australian Higher Education', *Cambridge Journal of Education*, vol. 41, 2011, pp. 5–22

Rowe, E., Lubienski, C., Skourdoumbis, A., Gerrard, J. and Hursh, D., 'Templates, Typologies and Typifications: Neoliberalism as Keyword', *Discourse*, vol. 40, 2019, pp. 150–161

Santos, B. de S., 'If God Were a Human Rights Activist: Human Rights and the Challenge of Political Theologies', *Law, Social Justice and Global Development Journal*, vol. 1, http://go.warwick.ac.uk/elj/lgd/2009_1/santos

Schippert, C., 'Implications of Queer Theory for the Study of Religion and Gender: Entering the Third Decade', *Religion and Gender*, vol. 1, 2011, pp. 66–84

Schwartz, B., 'The Social Context of Commemoration: A Study in Collective Memory', *Social Forces*, vol. 61, 1982, pp. 374–402

Scott, M., Murphy, E., and Gkartzios, M., 'Placing "Home" and "Family" in Rural Residential Mobilities', *Sociologa Ruralis*, vol. 57, pp. 598–621

Shanahan, M. (ed.), *Does Religious Education Matter?* (London: Routledge, 2017)

Smith, K., 'Producing Governable Subjects: Images of Childhood Old and New', *Childhood*, vol. 19, 2001, pp. 24–37

Smyth, E., Lyons, M., and Darmody, M. (eds), *Religious Education in a Multicultural Europe* (Basingstoke: Palgrave 2013)

Todd, S., 'Educating Beyond Cultural Diversity: Redrawing the Boundaries of a Democratic Plurality', *Studies in Philosophy of Education,* vol. 30, 2011, pp. 101–111

Tweed, T.A., *Crossing and Dwelling: A Theory of Religion* (Cambridge, MA: Harvard University Press, 2006)

Tyler, I., 'Classificatory Struggles: Class, Culture and Inequality in Neoliberal Times', *The Sociological Review*, vol. 63, 2015, pp. 493–511

Valentine, G., 'Living with Difference: Reflections on Geographies of Encounter', *Progress in Human Geography*, vol. 32, 2008, pp. 323–337

van der Kooij, J.C., de Ruyter, D.J., and Miedema, S., '"Worldview": The Meaning of the Concept and the Impact on Religious Education', *Religious Education,* vol. 108, 2013, pp. 210–228

van Krieken, R., 'The "Best Interests of the Child" and Parental Separation: On the "Civilizing of Parents"', *The Modern Law Review,* vol. 68, 2005, pp. 25–48

Weisse, W., 'RedCo: A European Research Project on Religion in Education', *Religion and Education*, vol. 37, 2010, pp. 187–202

Wilcox, M.M., *Queer Women and Religious Individualism* (Bloomington: Indiana University Press, 2009)

Williams, A., Cloke, P., and Thomas, S., 'Co-constituting Neoliberalism: Faith-Based Organisations, Co-option and Resistance in the UK', *Environment and Planning*, vol. 44, 2012, pp. 1479–1501

Yuval-Davis, N., 'Power, Intersectionality and the Politics of Belonging' (FREIA Working Paper Series, 2011), http://vbn.aau.dk/files/58024503/FREIA_wp_75.pdf

Zelizer, V., *Pricing the Priceless Child: The Changing Social Value of Children* (Princeton, NJ: Princeton University Press, 1985)

Index